Forward Press Poets 2009

Expressions From The UK

Edited by Forward Press Editors

First published in Great Britain in 2009 by:
Forward Press
Remus House
Coltsfoot Drive
Peterborough
PE2 9JX
Telephone: 01733 890099
Website: www.forwardpress.co.uk

Foreword

Here at Forward Press our aim has always been
to provide a bridge to publication for as many
undiscovered poets as possible. We firmly
believe that poetry should be accessible to all
and most importantly should connect with
the reader. Over the past 21 years we have
published a hugely diverse range of poems from
writers young and old, creating anthologies
that celebrate the wealth of writing talent on
offer. With the inclusion of both traditional
rhymes and more modern verse, there is always
something to suit everyone's tastes.

This latest collection of poems written with
creative flair and a passion for the local area
is sure to engage and entertain. We hope
you agree that Forward Press Poets 2009 -
Expressions From The UK is one to treasure and
return to time and again.

Contents

The Poems

The Skimmer

Standing still
At the water's edge
A skimmer in my hand

Smooth and thin
With a flinty rim
Gnawed by the teeth of time

Remembrance
Then sent it skimming
Across a mirrored sky

Once, twice; thrice
Illusion it grazed
Which opened and swallowed

Splintering
The blue sky, it fled,
Leaving waves in its stead.

Ellen Dwyer

My Love

You lift my heart
With your smile,
The touch of your hand,
Your body against mine.

Your face lights as
It sees mine;
You call my name -
Yes, my love,
My grandchild,
I am here.

Barbara Bowen

Madeleine McCann
(Missing in 2007)

Gripped as a nation
We hope and we pray
For the little girl missing
Since the 3rd of May

A Mother and Father's torment
On that fateful day
When their dear little Madeleine
Was taken away

Their beautiful little girl
With her teardrop eye
Her face never forgotten
As time goes by

For Madeleine McCann
The search still goes on
Her parents so tired
But their fight still so strong

Her parents wouldn't have left them
If they'd have known
One day I hope they'll find her
And bring her back home.

Kelly Gosney

Gone

When I look out of my window
You would think I'd see the view of my garden
But what I really see is what's in my mind
Many things in my mind are always left unfinished
I'd start trying to imagine what my eldest sister
Looks like . . .
I always started imagining the face, eyes, hair but
Then suddenly it would disappear
I'd then try to imagine what sort of things she would
Be doing in life
I'd always thought she would make it to one of the
Top unis doing a high-class job
Again, the thought would disappear
Like I say, the business of my imagination is always . . .
Left unfinished
The only thing I find hard is when she died
Where did she go?
They say she went to Heaven and is going to be reborn again
They say she is in good hands with God
Is there a God?
In my mind I do think she is watching over me
Every step of the way
Wherever she is in the world, I'd never forget her
And I'd always be thinking of her every second of the day
Every night I'd still shed a tear for her
For happiness as well as my grieving
Wherever she is, may peace be upon her . . .

Poonam Gogna

The Poet

The power of poetry, a chronicling of experiences that bring pleasure or pain.
Specifically arranged words that when seen or heard will stimulate the brain.

To look upon humanity and lyrically describe everything within your vision.
Connecting with strangers as the poet imparts their insight into
                                                    the human condition.

A poem about love and joy with an arcane resonance that makes sensitive
                                                    hearts soar.
A poem to condemn the evil in our world, infused with optimism that when we're
knocked down lifts us from the floor.

Poetry is simply an expression of what we all think, of the feelings in some way or
another that we all feel.
For most it's all too big for them to express, an elusive fantasy until another takes
those thoughts and makes them real.

Poetry says here is someone else who understands the highs and lows of life.
As others struggle to make sense of it the poet writes words that cut through
                                                    like a knife.

When the most mundane events are made fresh and exciting by a beautiful
                                                    turn of phrase.
When tired eyes look again at day to day existence and once more have wonder
                                                    in their gaze.

A creative spirit seeking expression, searching for the words that will take a
troubled mind and raise it higher.
The flesh turns to dust but the essence remains upon the page and in
                                                    everyone they inspire.

Humbly offering some solace, a piece of the writer that anyone can forever keep.
Voices from the distant past with a message to hold to when the going gets steep.

So when things seem bleak, when the darkness threatens to swallow you whole,
Remember the power of words and let poetry be the medicine for your soul.

John Burton

Our Garden

So proud the pine, so rich the copper beech,
We found a plum tree, apples, pears and peach,
Hidden paths all overgrown and wild,
But sheer enchantment for a little child.

No longer sad, neglected and forlorn,
Soon our three babies toddled on the lawn,
They had their birthday parties, climbed the trees,
Did cartwheels on the grass and grazed their knees.

The pond, the swing, blackberries and the shed,
The rabbits and the hamster to be fed,
The cat, the dog, all snoozing in the sun,
Water play and sand pies, it was fun!

The flowering cherry burst with pink delight,
Daffodils, bluebells, wallflowers, what a sight,
Bedding plants ablaze with summer's glow,
Delphiniums, lupins, roses, such a show.

Bonfires, fireworks in the autumn mist,
Beneath our home-grown mistletoe we kissed,
To Harvest Festival we took our runner beans,
Our apples, pears and plums could all be seen.

And suddenly, it was our Silver Wedding,
Just as autumn trees began their shedding,
All arranged, a marquee on the grass,
Family grown up, how time had passed.

Within our garden we found joy and peace,
A warm contentment that would never cease,
How fitting that beneath our lovely trees,
With sadness and with love I placed your wreaths.

But in our garden you are very real,
And by the grace of God, this heart will heal.

Valerie Geller

The Song Of Saturday's Outing

By the shore of windy Lowestoft
On the cliffs *this* side of the lighthouse
Dwells Hermione (neé Taylor)
Benjamin, her husband, with her
Gray, the charming couple's surname
One fine morning to Great Yarmouth
(Noisy, vulgar, haunt of trippers
Fish and chips their staple diet)
Came this pair in search of Sainsbury's
Tempted by some tasty offer
Sadly, Sainsbury's proved elusive
But the trusty Marks and Spencer
Sandwiches for lunch provided
Chicken was the lady's fancy
He in richer prawns delighted
Where to eat them was the problem
But so dire their pangs of hunger
To a crowded bench they hurried
In the market place adjacent
Hoping they would not be spotted
By some group from nearby Lowestoft
He was flanked by a large woman
Plus a bottle-sucking baby
She was perched upon the arm-rest
Avidly, they started eating
But, ah me, a sudden mishap!
As she moved with eager footsteps
To annexe a vacant corner
Down some chicken fell before her
Ripe for a small boy to slip on
Ah, her shame and oh, her sorrow
('Master' stayed aloof, unhelpful)
But how often, in such moments
Of distress, a canine helper
Like some deus ex machina
Solved our problem, he just ate it
Back they came, the ordeal over
Down the A12 heading southwards
To the safety of their dwelling

Thankful now that none had seen them
They could laugh at their adventure
By the shore of windy Lowestoft
As they watched a golden sunset
From the cliffs, *this* side of the lighthouse.

Caroline Buddery

I Need You Back

I wonder why my back went out
I wish it had stayed in
For now I'm shuffling about
On four-hourly aspirin.

I wonder why my muscles scream
With great enthusiasm
And now I'm rubbing in heat cream
With every knotted spasm.

I wonder why I'm stiff and sad
Just mumbling with this pain
I only know that I'll be glad
When my back comes in again!

Jenny Springett

My Thoughts

My thoughts are my own
They arrive unedited
Uninvited, unannounced, they just turn up
No caution, distortion or need for abortion
My thoughts are my own
Exempt from rule, regulations and morals
Yours, society's, my brother's and even my mother's
They are mine, the only things that truly are
Even the children with my genes, my sustenance
Fed, grown, nurtured, released
Not mine
My thoughts are my own
I didn't think they needed protection
Don't see why they are under objection
Innocent, without design, no planning involved
Not like your words
Created to chip, split, maim and shame
Was that judgemental?
Manufactured, fractured, broken when spoken
Morphed into a bullet-like token
From notion to word, man-made
A simple thought, I wish it had stayed
Corrupted between brain, hand and pen
Twisted, tangled, completely mangled
You see, my thoughts were my own
Now they are for you
Foolish, foolish me!

My thoughts are my own
Once I stupidly said them out loud
Defected, inspected, returned infected
My thoughts are my own, un-ejected.

K Scarfe

Painting The Sky

Arcs of colour traverse the sky,
As if a hint of magic is in the air.
I know there's a perfectly logical explanation
But it's fun to imagine who could have put them there.

Maybe a giant was feeling artistic,
And set to work with brushes and paints;
Using the sky as his personal canvas,
Expressing himself freely, without constraints.

Could a fairy have waved a wand,
Closed her eyes and made a wish;
Chuckling to herself as she noticed
The vivid colours appearing in a single swish?

And is it really true what they say,
Do you find a pot of gold at the end of the rainbow?
I'd like to believe it but I've admitted defeat,
My search has proved fruitless, perhaps I'll never know.

Annabelle Tipper

Primary Morning

Newly wakened, lively
pupils bustle into the hall,
with windows ceiling to floor,
where long searching rays ride
slanting through curtained gaps
as Earth bends ever slowly
to greet the rendering sun.

a miracle re-made
unfolds a beginning day
echoing the first morning,
gifting a fresh affirming
to carry old stains away;
deep promises for all construed,
sweet chances to create renewed.

J Stephen

Diamonds In The Snow

Come, walk with me
And see . . .
Diamonds in the snow.
Glittering, perfect jewels of light
Set in crisp snow on someone's front lawn.
Look . . .
So many of them . . . over there . . . over there.
The longer I stand
The more I see.

A delivery man returning from the house
Causes me to voice my wonder and
Exclaim my reason for standing there:
Look. . . diamonds in the snow.'
'Better grab 'em quick. It's the Credit Crunch,'
Comes the stark reply.

Left alone, I look again . . .
The jewels now like tiny fairy lights,
Lit by the low afternoon sun.

What price these jewels?
A little time to look.

But quick,
They will not last.

Yes, they will.
I'll put them in the casket of my memory,
And take them home.

Margaret Holden

The View From The Hill

We now look down on
The view from the hill,
Everything is still there
In its place, nothing has
Been changed by time,
Only in the faces of
The young and the old,
Memories etched in their
Smiles, warm as summertime.
The buildings weathered by
The passing four seasons,
The lighthouse, now unused
But still standing firm, tall,
The white sails of the boats
Ruffled by a sea breeze,
Nearby the golden corn is
Waiting for the harvest time,
Once by the hand scythe now
Rotating blades of a combine,
Revolving around like all our
Memories, that return into
Place, while our moment's
Recaptured, looking down
At the view from the hill.

Steven Pointer

Landlubber Cat

Cat lazy lounging on sun-cocooned dock wall
Licking lips fine fish supper thoughts
Drooping weary head onto paws
Now deaf to the workings of folk at sea
Falling asleep and beginning to dream.

Suddenly ship's bow rising like a high speed lift
Crashing down into foam-filled steel grey trough
Spray lashed figures clinging to the net on the winch
Hauling inboard cod laden catch released
Oil skinned sea booted men now gutting, swearing.

Bridged 'Old Man' sonar encompassed, ship's wheel besieged
Cursing and sweating alone with wind howled ship yawing, rolling
Gutting crew, sucking fish livers to relieve dry mouths
Restless ship's cook bringing up steaming home mugs
Tired sinew and bone soup and freshly baked body warming buns.

Cat rolling, yawning, falling to ground
Recovering, stretching, shaking free
Head empty of mice and foul-smelling rats
Looking for the fresh sea-fresh fish
Now sailing back to innocent shore.

Richard Cotterill

The Tall Ship

Pirate, unchain me from these chains of convention
That choke and stifle,
Brandish your sword for my freedom,
Wipe my sweating brow
With the bandana from your long, flowing hair
That blows so gracefully on the sea salt air.

Unfurl the sails, let the cannon yawn,
While the whole wide world looks on in scorn.
Let the look-out high above in the crow's nest
Beat a cool tune upon his broad breast.

Let the crew weigh anchor, let us depart.
Away, away from this restricting port,
Away from the chains in which we are bound,
In search of the homeland we've never yet found.
To sail to the ebb and flow of the tide,
Only pirate prince, stay close by my side.
To answer the call of the sea - far off - to set sail

To beyond the horizon.

Anita Challis

Goodbye

Nobody knew he had gone
Until they found his keys
Tucked into the pocket
Of his son's jacket
Hanging on the red peg
In the nursery cloakroom.

Susan Maclennan

Secret Thoughts

I need you now
So please don't shout
I'm drowning in my thoughts
Unable to grasp what's happening
How lonely and wanting
To be held with love
How I wish you wouldn't shout

I'm shouting again
But wish I wouldn't
Unable to grasp what's happening
You're sitting huddled with hidden expression
How lonely I feel, perhaps I hate you now
Stop looking at me with those beautiful eyes
Looking now realising I love you
How I wish I wouldn't shout.

Ann Bell

Eternity

Now that I am dead and in the earth
I write this from the grave,
In that it might find usefulness
Some poor sad soul to save.

For when I reached the river Styx
The boatman waited there,
He fixed me with his baleful gaze
And held me with his stare.

No sound he made, no question asked,
But his manner seemed to say,
I am awaiting your instruction,
For you have to choose the way.

Heaven or Hell, which one is it?
You make the choice you see.
But remember when you do that
It is for eternity.

There are idyllic days of sweet content,
If we drift downstream.
Lazing idly in the sun
With nothing to do but dream.

But, if we go the other way
Fires of Hell will burn your soul.
For excitement, lust and debauchery
Are in the Devil's bowl.

Look back upon your time on Earth
For it is there the answer lay,
And when you see which path you choose
Then you must point the way.

Hearing these words I was filled with dread.
There will be no rest for me
For I must face the Devil's wrath,
For all eternity.

So those of you I've left behind
Seek redemption if you can.
For your turn will come to answer
When you meet the ferryman.

Barney S Smith

That's A-Plenty

(Provoked after seeing two television adverts - one following the other - one for Oxfam and the other for a supermarket)

Come - my little bag of bones,
While you are able - let me take you by the hand,
And shepherd you around one of our many maze-like supermarkets,
To explore our irresistible range of tortured foods.
Here we have choice, oh, what a choice -
A harvest of plenty, even of delicacies out of season.
Some, perhaps from your own impoverished land.
Why look! Even our pets are provided for in so many ways.

Oh! My little washboard ribs, you are overcome.
Let me carry you, you weigh so little.
Your eyes are tired and you dawdle so.
Better still, let me trundle you in this trolley
While we tour these burdened rows of food-filled fancies.
Observe the varieties, since every desire is catered for.
Every bewitching shelf contains variations on a theme
Of seducing luxury, of selected goods on special offers.

Unfortunately - where there are so many alternatives,
Regretfully there will be waste, the law demands date regulation.
However, the welfare of our customers must come first.
Observe, as we pass these suffering shelves, the colourful
Displays, the mouth-watering pictures that enhance our
Products, some of which, sadly, date up, will be disposed of.

And now, my weary undernourished child, you must return
To your Third World. Do not forget to relate to them
The wonders you have seen, and the many superstores
Filled with 'must have' desirables and preferences.
Tell, of your pre-visit to Heaven. Will they believe you?
Will they believe that there are those, who not content with
Regular meals, are enticed to indulge between feasting?
No, they will only believe, that overcome with hunger,
You have dreamed delirious dreams.
                    Think of us with our daily dilemmas.

John Barns

The 'Movie' Invention

The man who invented moving stills,
Collaborated stories to vanquish our ills,
Then sound was added away from the screen,
To make sure that actors could speak and be seen.
This phenomenon then started sweeping the States,
Fortune and fame took their place in the stakes.
A new town named 'Hollywood' was suddenly born,
For creation and comfort and a sparkling new dawn.
With screen colour added, reality had come
To a fictional tale that was second to none.
Audiences thrilled as the stories unfolded,
But the film stars and fashion were rarely upheld!
No one remembered 'The old movie queen',
For their act was to vanish, no more to be seen.
Now time has run forward and slowed down a pace,
But the famous still tarry to keep in the race.
They take time with make-up and costumes to see
Their last avid sound bite on the TV!
For the movies no longer set up actors to fall,
But statesmen and salesmen have affected us all!

Christine Flowers

Come! Dance With Me!

We had a favourite holiday destination.
Every moment we could spare -
We rushed north up to Blackpool,
Because the Tower ballroom was there!

If you haven't flickered in a quickstep,
Floated dreamily in a foxtrot haze.
Swooped and lunged in a tango,
It's time you changed your ways!

The beautiful painted ceiling,
In summer, open to the air,
The music from the Wurlitzer organ
Made you feel you were in Heaven there!

A quiet flat in St Annes
Overlooking the little park.
Gave us everything a holiday should have -
It really 'hit the mark'.

The English weather couldn't spoil it.
The exercise could do nothing but good.
We've become too old to pursue it -
But, how we wish we could!

J M Jones

A Rite Of Spring

Erect now the maypole!
Let's dance the rite of spring
And celebrate the lust for life
This season always brings.

The cherry blossom pink and white
Around which the bees now hum
Proclaim the future bounty
That in summer soon will come.

Young bucks strut their stuff
In front of blushing maids
While older folk their arms entwined
Recall those happy days.

Erect now the maypole!
Let's dance the rite of spring
And celebrate the love of life
This season always brings.

Paul George

Of Peace

Peace is a mystery,
Of Christ's face, as
Of an infinity, He divines
The world, into a peace, that never ceases;
To clarify the moment of joy
In the soul of a bewildered man,
Lost in the wilderness of the universes
Of galaxies, sometimes non-understandable, in their very
Ingenuity, engineering and power; peace is
In the almighty revolution
Of the presence of the spirit,
Of Christ, as He heals our conscious,
Like the split second
Of a snowflake, patterning,
And falling, snow on snow,
Intrinsic design, pattern of grace.

And comprehending, Man perceives the visual
Spirit of Christ, transcendentally,
Re-patterning Man's body and soul
Into healing, humanity;
Like as the sun reflects and
Deepens, the depth and height of a mountain,
Reflecting, in mountain light, on the flowing lake below,
Revolving, and dazzling in green, mossy, radiant blues,
Around deep, black rocks;
How awesome, yet such joy,
Within Man's soul.

Yet now, as we gaze
Upon the face of a rose
In the morning,
The beauty of which
Can never be destroyed, such joy, such freedom.

This, the vision of the
Presence of God,
The sublime, of humanity and love,
Stretching, through eternity,
Within the body and soul,
Linking, century to century, vital with life,
This is the point of

The love of God, to free mankind;
One of the greatest gifts on Earth,
Like as a ball,
Bounced in a kindred spirit,
We are free;
Like the poetry of a fine couple's cooking,
Providing grace and bread,
Kneaded, baked and risen,
And given in love, with a fish,
As communion of awareness,
That poetry of all poetry,
To bear us back to life,
From the dark,
To the face of Christ,
Adored, and reverenced,
To free Man in work,
To creative giving,
Oh, symbol of peace on Earth;
Like the balance of a man,
Trapezed, on the tip of a mountain peak.

E R French

Invocation

Thy will be done . . .
Only, Lord, speak loud and clear,
For we cannot hear You above the roar of traffic,
The shrill, desperate laughter and the clatter of teacups.

Thy will be done . . .
Only we are always so busy,
Keeping up payments and appearances,
Being popular, witty and shrewd.

Peace be on Earth . . .
After the last bomb has fallen,
The last shot has been fired
And the last catty remark has been made.

G Birke

To Linda

One day we went to London town
To a church near Paddington Green,
To attend a day-long festival
And in the leisure time between,
We walked by a canal, quite near,
The 'Little Venice' so-called there.

Another day in London town,
We went to see the sights;
Big Ben and England's parliament,
Where laws are made for people's rights;
And then within the ancient tower,
To see the jewels, queued an hour!

We took a ride on river bus
And took our seats without a fuss;
We passed the dreaded Traitor's Gate,
Where once sad men bemoaned their fate:
Past wharves and warehouses we sailed,
Beneath a bridge where Daphne paled,
But said to Linda, 'This is fun,'
Lest we both became undone!

In Kensington's wide gardens' span,
We saw the famous Peter Pan,
And the round pond, where many a boat
By breeze and sail was kept afloat;
And girls and boys had come to play
Over the years for many a day.

Then one weekend we went to stay
At Malling Abbey, old and grey:
Passed 'neath the gatehouse where the knight
Who killed St Thomas made his flight
For sanctuary, there he fled
From the king's wrath, in mortal dread:
The ancient guest house where we stayed,
Once horses 'neath the guest rooms neighed:

Now you're grown up and I am old,
But when this little tale is told,
We will remember those bright days
As happy memories always;
When we went up to London town
And down to Kent where hops are grown.

Daphne Foreman

Congratulations

C lever of you to thrive so long
O dds on you'll still be here
N inety and nine years from today
G rowing in size by the year
R emarkable fame you are gathering too
A chieving such dreams for us folks
T urning our thoughts to reality
U nleashing our wishes and hopes
L etting us reach our ultimate goals
A nd seeing our own words in print
T housands of folk are grateful to you
I ndeed to us you're the 'mint'
O ffice staff too do a wonderful job
N oting our spelling mistakes
S potting each verse that's worthy of print
   Congrats! You all take the 'cake'!

Elsie J Sharman

It's Good To Talk

What makes your brow so furrowed?
What makes your eyes so sad?
What worries lie beneath your smile?
Can it really be that bad?

A smile that does not reach your eyes
No sparkle, nothing's there
But fear and disillusionment,
You pretend that you don't care.

Sometimes we need perspective,
Another's point of view
To help sort things out in our head,
To get the happiness we're due.

Just talk to me, just let it out,
I won't judge or criticise you,
I'm just a friend who wants to help,
I've felt the same way you do.

So glad you could confide in me,
Why did you wait so long?
To get these feelings off your chest,
To tell me what was wrong.

So, now you can be happy,
Put the past behind and smile,
A smile that lightens up your face,
One I've not seen for a while.

Jo Miller

What Of A Tear

Hell's gates are open
For those who cannot cry
For without emotion
Life will pass you by
A man who cries is called a sissy
By those who don't understand
It's communication through emotion
Talking through your eyes
Tears can express more joy
Than words can ever hope to convey
Or show deep down grief
When sadness comes your way
One tear is but a drop
In a mighty sea
Yet a tear could change the world
And not get a mention in history.

P Maidment

Blue Against Chrome (2)

As I look into the night, and catch a glimpse of bright moonlight
Reflecting from your glass and chrome, I gaze, at your new a la mode,
Such symmetry of lines and curves, in contrast to surrounding modes,
You stand so proud, with grandeur formed, from architectural imagery.

If I should look another way, I'd see a name upon a grave,
A name that brought me to your door, the creator, of one Eleanor,
Side by side, with those whom shared a life, of poverty at best,
All weathered now, you lay beneath the ground, entombed, but now at rest.

Withstanding not on protocol, from visitors, who leave so much more
Than that, of which was given thee, for works, once give oh so free,
I wonder what there might have been, if wealth, that you had truly seen,
Or whether poverty and strife, added to your spice for life.

As day replaces night so slow, and sunlight penetrates the mode,
Thy shadow casts a replica, of that which passed in dawns before,
Yet as you stand so proud and tall, I wonder, how many will recall?
Your structure, and proximity, and thus; why now I know of thee.

Robert Maguire

The Flower Arranger's Nightmare

Her festival arrangement was not a howling success.
The oasis all floated to the top of the vase,
Definitely not one of her best.
It was meant eventually to depict The Festival of Light
But though she tried and rammed 'em in hard,
The damn thing still wouldn't go right.
So, when a county voice exclaimed
'Aiy saiy, I thought the theme was light,'
She replied, as her patience expired -
'*It is* - this is a hedge on a very dark night.'

Joan Hurren

I Will Always Love Her

Now those fallen leaves
Are everywhere
Tell me if she's there
In the arms of another

While we're apart
I'll be wishing
I was close to her heart
As I will always love her

And wherever she goes
I do hope she knows
Just how much I love her

Now those fallen leaves
Are everywhere
Tell me if she's there
In the arms of another

While we're apart
I'll be wishing
I was close to her heart
As I will always love her.

K Lake

Thought For The Day

Today's a day - no matter where,
This day God gave for all to share,
How different though in circumstance
Through incident, or birth, or chance
To each of us the day appears
To some all smiles - to others tears.

The day you made it to the top,
Or the day you saw your efforts flop,
The day ambitions were achieved,
Or the day you lost and sadly grieved,
A day you hoped and tried and planned,
A day you held a loved one's hand.

Today's a day, no matter where,
This day God gave, for all to share,
Today's a day for me, and you,
Cherish it and see it through,
But count your blessings ere it's past,
For today has but a day to last.

Joyce Barker

Music Of Time

The sun dances a samba
With his shadow wife,
Through high-stepping branches
On the brown and amber ballroom
Of last year's leaves.

When we dance on the dead
As we must, may we not grieve
But accept this flickering life
Always alters but never disappears.
Summer to winter, round and round,
Ground to leaf, leaf to ground.

Gillian Bence-Jones

Transience

Oars rising, oars dipping
The queen of the marshes
Cannot sleep
The queen of the lagoon
Floats awake
Across the maze of canals

Oars dipping, oars rising
The queen of slate green waters
Digs deep into the bricks
The queen of aged beasts
Slithers and prowls and flies
Across piazzas, palazzos and tides

Rise of tides, fall of tides
The queen of the silver sea
Guilds arches and columns
The queen of darkness
Vaults banners over bridges
Across dreams pulled taut by the wind.

Mariana Zavati Gardner

Society

If I could heal and cure all ills,
Where would I begin?
Would it be in the hearts of men
And all their kith 'n' kin?

Just look at the children, to make a start,
That's enough to break your heart!
How does one reconstruct thought?
That is something that cannot be bought!

Save our souls from our own brethren
And from 'fanatics', for God's sake, sever them!
But here we go again
Travelling down the same old lane.

I feel for some that it's a crime
But we are quickly running out of time.
Show me a person who is strong
And I will show you one who's wrong.

For strength in body, is *not* soul,
This brute strength does not make 'whole'.
Must we waste *all* that we've been given
To try to prove that we are 'living'?

In this strange society
Full of impropriety,
How do we continue to be thus so?
Well, I must confess, I don't know!

Kathleen Kennedy

A Red Poppy

The old man stood with his poppy
In his buttonhole today
And as he stood at the memorial
His mind was far, far away.

The scrambling nets were hanging
To the landing craft below
And down he went with all his kit
To a future that he didn't know.

He remembered how he landed
On a little beach in France
He still could see the landing
As if he was in a trance.

Then he smelt the cordite of battle
As the 25 pounders roared
He saw the Shermans crawling
And the airborne whom he adored.

He saw the streets of Bayeux
Where he saw the first of the French
Then into the bocage country
With death and cattle and stench.

He spent his time mortar spotting
With radar to give him a hand
While the guns were used in field role
And not anti-aircraft as planned.

He stayed till the Normandy breakout
Through the Falaise gap and the Seine
He saw the dead German soldiers
The thousands that still there remain.

But now his mind started to falter
He had tried to forget this for years
As he glanced up at the memorial
His eyes were just filling with tears.

So we come to the end of the story
May we all hope and pray wars will cease
Will nations be friends now forever
And the poppy a simile for peace?

R Smith

The Met

I woke up fuming yet again
For where was all the promised rain?
I settled back in sweet repose
And even packed away the hose.
They promised weather fine and sunny,
It poured with rain and wasn't funny.
I got soaked, I had no brolly,
All due to met man's forecast folly.
They blame it on the highs and lows
And where they're going, goodness knows!
Unsettled weather so they say,
We might even get some hail today.
The isobars are closing tight,
We'll have a gale force wind tonight
And if we dare to ask them why,
They bluff and say, 'It's in the sky.'
So up the garden path we are led,
For them to earn their daily bread.

Marie Wood

Carefree Days

'There's a fair in the meadow, come on and see
With swing boats and merry-go-round,
Get some coins in your pocket and follow me,
Sample the joys to be found.'
'Mind what you're doing,' our mothers would say
As we hurried off down the road.
'Don't buy any rubbish or get in the way,
Do as you're told and be good.'
With our money clenched in hot little hand
Or jingling around in a pocket
We'd head for the sound of the loud 'Louisa' band
Piped by piston, engine and sprocket.
A go on the hoopla, win a fish in a bowl
Or roll pennies down a wood ramp
With all sorts of people we'd meet cheek and jowl,
Sometimes even a tramp.
A ride on a roundabout all shiny with brass
With horses and cockerel all guilded,
In the sunshine sit on the grass
Tired, a little bewildered.
Bright coloured ice cream plopped in a cone
From a man pushing a trike,
Candyfloss, apple jack, here bees would drone,
All things sticky and gooey we liked.
The sound of music, shouts from the stalls
From showmen plying their wares,
A shy at coconuts with hard wooden balls,
Here was a life without cares.
At the end of the day, home we did trudge,
Our time and money well spent,
Sit in a chair too tired to budge,
So pleased and happy we went.

Bill Fisher

Lonely Hearts Column

I want a man who is handsome
I'll make no bones about that
And his figure must be trim
I can't stand a man who is fat.
He must be quite a mover
Who can show me he's really alive
When he takes me on the dance floor
For tango, waltz or jive.
He must be smartly dressed
Though not necessarily flash
And one thing most important
He must have plenty of cash.
And of course he must be mobile
With a nice big limousine
A Rolls would be right up my street
I could sit in the back like a queen.
And I'd like him to support me
In all I say and do
Knowing I'll always be right, so
He'll have no need to argue.
And of course he must be charming
With a pleasing personality
You must have several men like this
So please, send one along for me.

Miss Oldan Haggard

Give Me The Key

I cried for myself
As they took him away
'Guilty as charged'
I had heard them say

Now he's locked up
Give me the key
Forever I will gladly
Keep it with me

He invades my dreams
Controls my day
I have tried to forget
But there is just no way

Let him feel pain
For the souls he destroyed
Stolen futures
I am lost in the void

So please, give me the key
When you lock him away
Behind fences and walls
Where I hope he will stay.

Susan Hindle

Remember Elizabeth

Her cards to me in a drawer attending
the wishes and love of a year gone before
that I may recall the divine lending
of riches so fine that will live evermore.

Something told me on that day when we
hugged the news of joy impending
about a doubt that somewhere lay
that would disturb my soul for time unending

Haunted still by undeserving plight
as she fought to stem the unequal flow
honour me that her courage might
enable easing of life's woe

She'll know about that splendid goal
and the swimming feet with his mates so great
for her mark is there to console our minds
when sorrow shards attempt dictate

Sorrow the morn as my thoughts hold sway
over loving first born that once I knew
river flow my tears away
as golden past turns to blue

Grief blows the willows now
as memories propel me down the lane
and as I stumble the churchyard scene how
I long to call her name.

Barry Girling

Reflection

Who is that woman looking at me, I've not seen her before
She reminds me of the old lady who used to live next door

But that can't be right, visions rushing through my head
Because that old lady is long since dead

I'll have to get my glasses and see what I can see
Oh, sweet goodness, it's a mirror and it's me

Where has all the time gone, and my golden locks?
By the look of me now I'm not long for my box

I must get going out of this hospital bed
And do some exercise like the doctor said

Then, perhaps in a very short time
My reflection in the mirror will be quite sublime

What did I hear in my head, a voice say,
'When pigs do fly, that'll be the day!'

Alma Brace

Our Nation

Earthquakes, hurricanes, floods, raging thunders
Nature's warning there are too many disasters and blunders
Wars, global warming, animal extinction, deforestation
Look what's happening to our nation

Workers providing for their families, trying to make ends meet
Struggling to pay bills and put food on the table to eat
Elderly people at home shivering because it's too expensive
to turn on the heat
The unemployed and homeless searching around
Looking for jobs, but not many can be found
Under pressure and stress they look on in despair
Wondering if anyone will help them or really cares

Babies/children living in poverty
Some suffering in silence from the hands of cruelty
It's a crying shame, how children have to endure so much pain
Dying from abuse, neglect and starvation
Look what's happening to our nation

The uncaring, selfish, un-united will fall
While a caring, democratic, multicultural society,
can only rise above all
De-throne from your thrones
Help the workers who work their fingers to the bones
Pick up the people who fall to the ground
Don't look on them with scorn and frown
Help them who choose to turn their lives around

Dig out the greedy weeds
That drain our land's nutrients and suppress
our growing seeds
Help the people to reap and enjoy the fruits they grow
Then look what will happen as our nation flourishes
prospers and grows.

Susan Tate

Reason Why I Write?

Words flow more freely, from poised pen,
When hear the call, 'versed lines',
Especially from mild manic men,
On which sun often shines.

Rhyming phrases leap out so fast,
Once task is undertook!
Will mindset state forever last,
When well, I'll fill thick book!

For poetry's finest relief,
Of life's frustrating claws,
To whirling brains, it's my belief,
Only depressed times, pause!

My doctor friend has always said,
'Such writing's therapy,'
Better release than end up dead,
Bi-polar's tragic fee!

It's a harmless hobby, cheaply free,
All's needed, pen and pad!
Even when weather's wintry,
It prevents thoughts too sad!

It's all to do with chemistry,
Those juices in the brain,
If events disturb symmetry,
Such days can lead to pain!

If chance changes chemicals right,
Then blue skies all around,
That gives happiness, day and night,
Creative urges found!

Bob Edwards

My Garage

My garage no longer houses the car,
It's too full of everything else, by far.
Cupboards and tables, chests and chairs,
Bicycles, freezer and various spares.
Gardening tools are also in place,
Screwdriver, hammer and nails, just in case.
My son's electrical bits and pieces;
Material placed there just increases.
Balls and toys for the grandchildren to play,
Other things boxed and stored away.
One cupboard full of pots of paint,
But never the right one is my only complaint.
Compost, grass seed, fertiliser, flower pots,
A bundle of string in a tangle of knots.
Bits of wood and coils of wire,
You never know one day what you'll require.
The lawnmower rests there with extension lead,
All ready and waiting for work to proceed.
Bags of rubbish must go to the tip,
When the sun shines I will make this trip.
Some people have no garage or shed,
So where do they put all their stuff instead?

Desma Day

On Aldeburgh Beach

Silver under the moon
The sea lies quiet
Only the sighing of the waves
And the waking breeze
That shifts along the shore
Breaks night's deep contemplation
The air lies easily upon us
We are still, we listen to the sound
Heard since the start of time
Feel the sadness too of loss and longing
And the echo of the lost heart's
Beating.
Only the hand held open
And the soul laid bare
Can give us hope or peace
All we have left is faith and love
Our sanctuary among turmoil
A respite from the world's oppression.

J M Oliver

In Memory Of Hughie

(1960-2008)

As I sit here and think of you
I feel so sad about it, Hugh
The day your sister came to say you'd died
I was dumbfounded, I cried and cried
How can someone beautiful and immaculate just go?
I don't understand, how would I know?
You were my ex husband and dad to beautiful Claire
She is the sparkling light that we both share
Please forgive me for not seeing you before you went
I just never thought soon you'd be Heaven sent
I hope you're watching from the sky above
To see our daughter marry her true love.

Christine Frances Williams

The Fox

Cackling from the hen house rose on the cool night air,
The torch beam stabbing through the dark,
Who knows what was lurking there!
The dustbins lidless and overturned,
Their contents strewn around,
The plastic bags all ripped apart,
Rubbish on the ground.
The moon emerged from behind the clouds,
Casting an eerie light,
A shadow appeared but briefly,
Then melted into the night.
The merciless light of morning
Showed evidence of the kill,
Feathers floating on the breeze,
The raider had taken his fill.
The carnage left behind him
Made it very plain
Who the perpetrator was,
The fox had struck again!

Jean E Reynolds

A King From Legend

And Raedwald came.
His horse halted as he took in the scene.
Shadows filled the night, an aura of mystery hovered.
Battleworn he lingered, longing to be enveloped by his people.
The Great Hall beckoned.
Already he felt warmth wrap around him like a great blanket.
Torches flamed.
Through the wispy trails of eerie smoke
Familiar faces shone in the light of the fire.
Merriment echoed all around him.
The adornments on his clothes dazzled
And the fighting helmet he carried blazed.
The lyre soothed.
Golden mead flowed with the stories -
The perilous sea, far away lands and entanglements.
Treasures spilled across the table in a tumble of gold and silver.
And in a corner
There was regality and majesty and salvation.
His wife.
Raewald had come home.
There was merriment and joy.

Margaret Delf Newson

An Urgent Message

Why are people not being told
Of how their destiny will unfold?
It is freely available for all to read,
What can be done to make them heed?
God made a covenant in a land far away
And this promise is still valid today.
His chosen man was called Abraham,
And later confirmed by His Holy Lamb.

This enthralling story must be true;
It captivates life in every hue.
Humanity shown throughout the ages
Is totally exposed within these pages.
A long awaited event took place -
The Son of God - a gift of grace
In a stable manger as a babe did lie;
Sent from Heaven - destined to die.

His example was a perfect life
Showing how to conquer sin and strife;
Finally he chose to endure great shame,
Nothing would ever be the same.
A trial without a guilty plea
Condemned Him to death upon a tree,
Then in a borrowed grave He laid,
The task fulfilled - the ransom paid.

Death did not win when Jesus died;
For mankind's sins he was crucified.
God welcomes Him back to Heaven's glory
And we inherited a mystery story.
Fast forward now from His time below,
The gospels foretell a time of woe;
So prepare for the day He will return.
Do read it now; there is much to learn.

A state of Israel has been proclaimed,
A universal leader will soon be named.
The nations assembling is foretold
A worldwide upheaval will unfold.
Read about it before time has flown
When we will be judged at Heaven's throne,
Each one to meet God face to face -
Just pray He will save you by His grace.

Joan Picton

Our Lifeboat Men

The cruel sea our brave men defy
Their tender hearts their deeds belie.
For tough on the outside they have to be
Tending the rescued their compassion you see.

They are a particular breed of man
Who face all odds, to help when they can
Those in danger at the mercy of the storm.
These men are not made, they are surely born.

At Caister-on-Sea we are truly blessed
With lifeboat men who have stood the test.
Dedication and courage they never lack.
Following their motto, 'They Never Turn Back.'

Helen Lock

A Year's Work

Gardening is like a nice good wine,
All shades of colour and flavours through time,
Winter's part is to sort and plan,
Research is vital for every man.
So much to choose, a lot to grow,
Every inch of ground to be covered I know,
With the choices made it's time to begin,
Spring is coming, get going to win.
Thousands of seeds ready to sow,
The garden is dug and ready to go,
All plants are up and they look great,
But planting out will just have to wait.
Now the frost has gone, it's warmer at last,
Everything is growing so very, very fast,
It's only the watering and weeding to do,
Flowers and veg have all come true.
My garden looks great; I've done real good,
Colourful and crowded as a good garden should,
Now is the time to pick, eat or store,
Clear the ground and start once more,
A good year I've had, it's time for a break,
So clean all the tools and put away the rake.

Pauline Glenister

The Fat Ballerina

Our Marilyn was born to dance,
From an early age she would skip and prance.
She twirled around so gracefully
And her pas de deux was a joy to see.

Then there came that dreadful day
When cream cakes and chocolate came her way.
As years rolled by, poor Marilyn
Grew older, heavier and far from thin.

With waning ambition and not so wise,
Marilyn grew to enormous size.
Her frilly tutu was far too tight
As she strained into it with all her might.

To find a partner was proving hard
And in Swan Lake her performance was marred.
Her dying swan looked all forlorn,
Like a dying duck in a thunderstorm.

So alas, poor Marilyn had to retire
And leave the ballet, complete with spare tyre.

Pauline Anderson

Early Risers

The morning chorus of the birds
Brings forth the break of day,
And the milkman trundling down the street,
As he wends his merry way.
The news boys and the news girls too,
With papers by the score,
All bleary eyed and weary too,
Push papers through the door.
All this goes on while we're asleep,
And much too tired to care,
But we would notice very soon,
If none of them were there.

Brian Chandler

Irish Dreams

I'm going to Ireland's emerald isle
Boarding a ferry, I'll be there in a while
My dream has come true, I'm in Dublin at last
To hear of the legends and the old Celtic past.

Tall mountains and hills looking so serene,
And rolling, green meadows, a velvety green.
Never-ending waters that go sailing past,
The journey ended, to the sea at last.

Watching the sheep grazing on rugged edges
And clever old goats balanced on mountain ledges
The heathers on the moors are a sight to be seen
And collecting of nectar where Mr Bee has been.

Strolling the lane for the man in green,
Leprechauns are heard but never seen,
Close my eyes and lo and behold,
He's sitting there counting his crock of gold.

Visiting old buildings from centuries past,
Climbing Blarney castle to kiss the stone at last.
Travelling home, it's now cold November
With wonderful memories I'll always remember.

J Merrick

Mouse

'Twas only a mouse though it was quite fat,
Eating some cheese that was bait for a rat,
His little coat gleamed as soft as silk,
For he'd just bathed in the pussycat's milk.

He was only a cat but he'd seen that mouse,
Whilst searching for the rat that was haunting the house.
The cat was portly but he'd spied a treat,
That mouse looked good enough to eat.

'Twas only a rat but he'd seen the cat,
And the mouse that had eaten his cheese,
Well, what a nerve both creatures had,
For rat was hungry if you please.

He was only a boy but a sporting one,
Who'd seen his chance to have some fun.
He watched as the cat, and the rat poised to pounce,
For a morsel of cheese that weighed, not an ounce.

It was only a balloon floating on a string,
But the boy had long tired of the thing,
It made such a bang that the cat, rat and mouse,
All chased that boy around the house!

C E Lally

Supermarkets? You Can Keep 'Em

I hate shopping at my local supermarket
The trolleys seem to have minds of their own.
I go up and down the gangways walking crabwise
Bumping people, I'm a walking danger zone.

And why is it people cannot see when you are coming?
I swear most of them seem to go out just to chat.
In groups of three or four, they block the blooming floor
Giving dirty looks, if I should prod a back.

And why do staff have to change the layout?
Cos the things I need are no longer there.
I get in such a flap, as I start another lap
Searching, ever searching - makes me swear.

Then, when it's my turn at the dreaded checkout,
Is the time the till roll's had enough.
Sally isn't able and has to call for Mabel
Who puts it right, but leaves her in a huff.

Of course, I'm the one with something minus barcode,
Which is when the eyes behind me start to bore.
If I had my own computer, my shopping list I'd booster
Then I wouldn't have to go there anymore.

A shopping trip for me is not a pleasure
There are things, or places I would rather be.
Somewhere nice and sunny - if I only had the money
Or watching TV, sipping cups of tea.

Gone are the days when you could write an order
For the corner shop, alas, who is no more.
I have a master plan - bring back that little man
Who aimed to please. And delivered to your door.

Alfred Revill

A Day At The Zoo

We love returning to Colchester zoo each year,
Travelling into the next county, oh, it's so near!
We visited the new orang-utan forest with 'Rajang' all alone,
Who had his fortieth birthday last year, a great milestone.

We then saw the mangabey baby hanging off his mother,
And both eating bread in the lovely mild weather.
We looked at four young kids, then stopped for a snack,
Planning the other feeding times, knowing we were well on track.

We queued patiently, Ashton dropped a carrot for the elephants,
And Taylor fed a giraffe, before seeing the ants.
Both our sons had their faces painted as a cheetah and a parrot,
Then we watched the chimpanzees eat such a lot!

We travelled on the Tanganyika road train to see more animals,
Afterwards our boys had a photograph next to the waterfalls.
Feeling tired from walking around, we still had energy to play,
And time to buy a gift to remember today.

Adrian Bullard

The Loneliness Of A Long-Living Lady

Sitting alone at the start of the day,
Washed, dressed and breakfasted in the usual way,
Wondering if anyone will happen to call
Or phone, or maybe, even a letter will fall
Through the letterbox, to just make my day
To possibly tell me a friend's coming to stay.

Sitting alone in the middle of the day
Hoping my neighbour may drop in to say
She has just made lunch and has some to spare,
Would I like to have some and just bring a chair,
To make conversation and hear all her news
And stay in her company as long as I choose.

Sitting alone at the end of the day
Knowing it is now too late and too grey
For a knock on the door to welcome a friend,
To sit for a while for a chat and extend
Goodwill and good cheer to lift up one's spirit;
So I suppose it's the telly and what's on offer within it!

I wonder if anyone will call tomorrow?

Cecilia Parrott

A Mother Lost

Mother loved dearly
Smile of warmth remains more now -
Than we care to remember.
Tenderness felt when needed most
Not just in memory with love as a mother -
Should be remembered.
This is not goodbye, rather farewell
Until we embrace again
Thoughts of you make the days lighter -
And the nights more welcome
Thank you for being there for us all
As the light welcomes your presence
Reunited with past loved ones
Sadness lingers with time
Though comforted, knowing
You rest in eternal peace
Dear Mother.

Alan Jones

The Flight

I board the plane to seek a better place
I need to break away from your familiar face
I must leave you for a while - take this flight
Leave homely substance and just take a case
I smile at my independence, knowing that this time is right.

Lives so entwined should give each other space
Within the hour, of me there is no trace.

The plane soars upwards out of sight
And soon has reached inestimable height
Its cargo full of every colour - race
Eager to land in some particular place
Some may be aware of taking fright
Our lives placed in someone else's hands
These hands steering us through the day and night
We feel the ground beneath us - now we land.

Huge flashings of great fire and light
The clang of fire engines rushing to our plight
Beating the flames they spray the metal bird
Within moments it's a pool of foaming white
And not a single person's voice is heard
The firemen had worked with all their might
A few survivors would recall their flight.

When watching birds take wing to emigrate
Filling the air with squawkings of delight and hope
Pause for a moment and just contemplate
That sometimes in our life we all just cope
Keep in your mind that some come late
That many will arrive at any rate
Some may never e'er return
However, they all wished to take their flight.

Pamela Gibson

The Night Of '42

The WWII bombing raids on Portsmouth and Southampton
Are well known, but just across the sea few knew, that
The Isle of Wight had its moment one night
In May 1942.

The raid on Cowes was quite sudden
One bomb fell near the family's back door
The blast blew it off its hinges
Knocking my grandfather to the floor.

Shrapnel smashed a large window
Passing through stairs into the floor
Where my infant brother had been sleeping
Just the afternoon before.

A house across the road was badly damaged
Grandfather heard a shout
He rushed over to help his neighbours
But the family were already wiped out.

He later returned, tired and exhausted
But on the rising of the sun
He saw a barrow, full of familiar objects
Looting had already begun.

For years after, when chatting at the gate
With locals, often when pruning his lilac tree, too
The subject would inevitably progress
To the night of '42.

Recently, my brother returned to the island
And once more walked up to see
The old family home. It was still there
So was the lilac tree!

Christine Plimmer

The Secret Track

Behind the crumbling old stone wall
Their first leaves beginning to fall,
Tall trees line the rutted track
Ancient trunks knotted and black.
Going downhill, woods on each side,
The lane is steep, not very wide.
Mildewed air is cold and dank.
Long grass hangs down either bank.
Turning, over a little bridge,
The track starts climbing up the ridge.
Woods thin out to grass and heath,
Fallen stones lying beneath.
The track has still one side of trees
Swaying now in the upland breeze,
Smaller now, and not so stout.
Over the top the path is green,
Walls and trees nowhere to be seen.
Heathland now, stretching away,
Golden in the warmth of day.
In the far distance, mountains rise,
Violet against the autumn skies.
Bracken scents the cooling breeze.
Soon enough white Winter's freeze
Will hide the track that leads up here
Until the springtime comes next year.

Haidee Williams

Well Oiled, But Still Rusting

I had a shovel and I had a pick
I kept a piece of string and piece of stick
I had a hammer, a chisel and a mate called Bob
Bob had tools as well

We placed in an advert our CVs to date
We mentioned the courses we'd taken and our certificates
In pointing and stacking and painting and all
And finished by stating *no job too small*

But no jobs were forthcoming, we had not one single true bite
The economy slowed and the money grew tight
One day with our loose change we made a joint speculation
Like millions of others we awaited congratulations

I still have a shovel, a pick and some string
These days I'm living the life of a king
I still meet up with Bob and his accountant son, Ted
While my tools hang, well oiled ,but still rusting
In my garden shed.

T S Harris

All My Yesterdays

Only seems like yesterday when champagne corks
Were popped with such elation
For my great birthday celebration!
What a wonderful day,
Never twenty-one again, never feel the same.
Time marches on 'they' say, but come what may
However old I grow, gratitude I'll show
For all my yesterdays.
Celebrate with me the enjoyment of each new year -
Trusting in Him who promises there is nothing to fear!

Shireen Markham

Precious Gift

Love is a precious gift
We give to one another
And when you're alone
Nothing matters but each other
But a secret love is something
That you treasure
Nothing can equal it, it can't be
Measured.

Holding each other, whispering
Dreams and hopes
Knowing deep down that your
Dreams have no scope
Knowing and dreaming can't make it
Come true
Just wishing there was no one
In the world but you two.

My love for you was always real
Where you are now
This I hope you still feel
You have left me empty
I couldn't say goodbye
My broken heart won't mend
No matter how I try.

Time they say heals all pain
But my heart won't be given
To anyone again
Knowing you as I did
Was a joy untold
Memories I have are precious
Like gold
So now rest in peace
Your troubles have vanished
And know my love for you
Will always be cherished.

S Mill

Special Angel (Tierna)

My beautiful daughter is special needs
And people say *poor you*
But we're really very lucky
If only people knew.
We're in the presence of an angel,
A gift from God above,
She hasn't any malice
Only happiness and love.
She gives each day a meaning
And taught us how to care,
Our lives would be so empty
If our angel wasn't there.
So next time you see a special child
Don't think or say *poor you,*
You're in the presence of an angel
And one of a chosen few.

Stella Branney

Wild Celandines

Beneath a beech hedge
Its leaves rattling their desiccation
A skirting of yellow

Gangly necked, upturned
Heads cocked toward a sun
Coy to reveal itself

An exuberance of its
Own making stark against
The penury of winter wear.

Ann Richards

War Breaks Out

Playing in the garden on a summer's day,
Walking in the park with my parasol so gay,
Picking dandelions and daisies by the score,
Only childhood pastimes, I did not wish for more.

Leslie was my boyfriend and always full of fun,
More than twelve years older and liked by everyone,
He'd run me on my trike racing round at tip-top speed,
Round and round the place we'd go, oh, that was fun indeed!

War was coming nearer, so the adults said,
Looking very solemn, they sadly shook their heads,
Evil was around us, they would have to fight,
Those summer days had given way to winter's night.

The boys came to the house to bid us all goodbye,
Smart in uniform they were, though some of them would die.
Leslie was a sailor now and soon had left the town,
Little did I know then that somewhere he would drown.

Father built a shelter in a garden bed
Caring for the family, to keep us safe, he said.
Soon the siren sounded, I was rushed there in the dark,
From the anti-aircraft firing in the park.

Soon the planes were zooming almost overhead,
Jerry ones were throbbing, would we all be dead?
Then our planes would chase them and so they flew away,
Back to bed we'd go, safe to face another day.

Judith Williams Francis

Eastertide

In life, nature fashioned me;
Through storm and calm
Through drought and flood,
Through hot and cold,
My anatomy was wrought,
Bedecked with foliage
Where birds and beasts had sanctuary,
While, underneath,
Love found a trysting place.

In green death, Man fashioned me;
With adze and axe,
With saw and plane,
Hammer and nail,
My new anatomy was wrought;
Two outstretched arms
Bearing sacrificial love,
Where the sick at heart find sanctuary,
While, underneath,
The restored a trysting place.

Thomas A Davies

To Be Good

It is important to be good or appear that way
Sensible in action, selfless in mind
Too good to be true some might say
So what in truth are we? That good?
I will be good to you, if you are good to me
Is motivation enough to reciprocate sentiment
But is my good bigger and better?
Requiring more thought, effort and energy
It does not matter, might be the cry
Have it on the house
You will feel better being a recipient
I will feel better basking in your pleasure
Or perhaps you will owe me?
In another way, I might not like the good that you are doing
If it involves spending time away
Doing good for others
It is for charity, it is voluntary, makes a statement
A loud exemplary statement of good
Contained and organised, political and bureaucratic and
Paid for, doing good
Then there is the good that is done in the name of war
Occupied and bloodied less valued are the opposition
In death
Unspoken killers are our heroes
Likeable, highly valued are our dead
Collateral damage are the innocent
But good and God are on our side
Doing good is not to be shared around
It is held close and tightly, by the chosen few
Leaving the rest, unsavoury, unclean dirty dogs and bastards.

Ron Constant

Just Because

In the valley
Where the children play
There lives a legend
As old as day
Like putting a peg
Upon the line
The sun sets black
Just for the blind
And as the wise man
Moved his lips to speak
No one could hear
Except the weak
For in hearing and in seeing
It all becomes quite clear
The reason and the being
Is just because
You're here.

Wilson E Jones

Tempus Fugit

And many a month and more and more,
The winds did blow, the rains did pour,
The world around me crumbled round
Each part of life was tumbling down.
As stress on stress o'ercame me so
I pledged with my eternal soul
If only I could get away
A break from torment day by day.
My need for help came ever near -
So life was weakening out of fear
I thought I could no longer hold
That tenuous thread to make me bold,
Instead I felt a time to go
Freedom from my constant foe -
At last a call - the quest was o'er
Respite from stress was at the core -
A need to get from enemy's thrall
His desire to take from me my all.
I see a light, though briefly bright,
If I could run into the sight -
I'd grasp those friendly arms and faces,
Thank God, at last, for all His graces.
My prayers are answered - long awaited -
Now my prayer is consecrated,
Sooner than later to return
Before I lose my life and home.
Take care, good friends, and ever thankful -
Life taken short - use well and thank you.

Sheila Redpath

Lest We Forget I Write To A Lad I Never Met

The sun is setting beyond the bay,
Casting a rosy glow upon the sea,
Snowdon's mountains reflect it back
As they stand in silent majesty,
And here I stand
In this windswept graveyard,
Part of Snowdon's lovely land.
The name upon the gravestone is of a lad I never met
A lad who'd played and grown amongst these peaceful hills
Sixty years have gone by, but I never can forget
His father's sorrow or his grieving mother's tears
As they stood amongst these fields and hills
And gazed down future years
When they would be without their loving son.
His body does not lie here in this silent, peaceful spot
Gnr Edward Jones, killed in an action long forgot,
His Mam and Tad now lie here beneath this monument
And the soft rains of Snowdon carry on their quiet lament.
I'm sure some other mother tends his grave
In that land so far away
And thinks about her children
Who also went away
Never to return.

Edward, I never met you but I'm sure you would agree
Never should we ourselves inflict this same grief on some other family,
Surely by now it's time we knew that killing never pays
Mothers everywhere just spend in grief all their remaining days.

Oh! Edward I never met you
I only knew your friends
They told me about the things you did and all your future plans
Hopes and dreams now laid to dust in that far-off, foreign land.

Yes Edward, I never met you but before I go away
I'll say a prayer for all who died
In that war so long ago
And on this quiet grave I'll lay
A solitary rose.

Mary Josephine Kerbey

Amazing Grace

Isn't God's grace amazing?
It's a wonderfully created thing

God does so many things we don't see,
Day in, day out, He's loving and changing me

I was a sinner but now I'm free,
Once was blind but now I see

Thank you, Lord, for Your amazing grace,
A glowing, powerful light glows around your palace

I love you more than words can say,
You love and care for me every day

You save me when I'm low,
You hold my head high when I'm feeling depressed or disliked
But you already know

You care for my life, help me to see,
It will be so amazing to see you in eternity

Thank you, Lord, for Your amazing grace,
That blesses in ways that have brought us to this place.

Beke Burgess

Serenading Masquerade

A tear,
Holds the volume of your betrayed love.
A second tear,
The screech of the flightless white dove.
The weeping heart,
Constellations of your eyes, switched off.
The sea of solitude,
The butterfly turned into the moth.
Looking back because now it seems so obvious,
The crashing of your crystal happiness.
Those rose petal glasses blocked out your senses
And you thought the rumour-mill
Was all run by cauldron wenches.
Rendering painful memory photograph flashbacks
Of your smitten expression up for public viewing.
How you bathed in the fiery emerald eye waters,
When probably they knew how your life was unglueing.
A fading picture of serenity,
The final sparks of electric energy.
One kiss,
Under the moonlit stratosphere.
One dance,
Under the sightless chandelier.
It all makes sense in retrograde,
When a hundred hearts went on parade,
With a thousand tears set to cascade,
And a million moments never to be made.
Emotional market where lovers trade,
He was your serenading masquerade.
She was your serenading masquerade.

Steven Howard

Night Eyes

There is a darkening
In all four corners
Of the night
As one by one
The stars go out.
Life has become
A heavy rolling train
On rusty line
And the future
Has stalled
In half murky light.
A comet stretched
Across an accusing sky
For a new home
In the sun,
Whilst dark angels
Of this Earth
Still sleep.

Norman Royal

Old Age

A wrinkled face peered at me through the window
And beckoned me in.
Soft footsteps were heard.
The door opened.

A thin skeleton, covered in sagging skin.
A worn-out body which had endured the two wars
And was nearing its end.

She made tea
And we drank.
I spoke of a world she didn't know
And she spoke of things that no longer existed.
She did not know that things had changed,
That streets were transformed,
Of people who died and generations born.

Time passed slowly, but eventually it was time to go.
I promised I would come again and saw myself out,
Through the iron gate that separated my world from hers.

I went to visit the old lady again, as I had promised.
I knocked - no one answered.
I looked through the window and there was nothing.

The old lady had reached the end of a rough, winding path.
I turned my back and walked into the street.
I leant on the iron gate.
It was cold and rusty and would soon crumble.

Avril Carnie

A Weary Winter

As weary winter lingers on and days pass oh so slow,
Not a working day in sight and nowhere left to go,
I do despair these hours away and long for better days,
I think of all the debts I owe and figure out the ways,
Who to pay or what to pay, I really don't know why,
When all I really can do is carry on and try;
And if this is not good enough, for each of those I owe,
Then sorry! Is all that I can say, whilst payments remain low,
And as for friends, you soon find out, those who do not care,
As only few will stay around, to share in your despair,
And even within our families, when we find ourselves in need,
We soon find out that only few will prove a friend indeed,
So if these weary winter days linger on a while,
Just carry on in your despair but, don't forget to smile,
For if you do when pounds are few, you'll find yourself alone,
And the friends you've got will drift away, if you moan and groan,
So just await that sunny day, with all your troubles gone,
And don't forget the ones who cared, as winter lingered on.

Ronald Simpson

A Peace Of Country

I wish I lived in the countryside
Where there's lots of places to run and hide,
Just in case I wanted to.
Sometimes I could if I felt blue:
In the long grass, up a tree,
Where no one can find me.
This is known as solitude,
Miles from nowhere, in a house of wood,
Then Dad, the boys 'n' the dogs got here.
My solitude was nowhere near.
It's really healthy when you're all around,
But this solitude I'd newly found,
Where are you, long grass?
Where are you, tree?
Where no one, can find me.
Where are you country house of wood?
You're holding all my solitude.

Caroline Connelly

All Through

Through guns and bullets yes! And roadside bombs
Through rain and fire, through traps and storms
Who knows what our soldiers do face?
An enemy there and difficult to trace
The Taliban of course, their terrorism but chase
But how far are they away?
As they only seek to kill day by day, and our boys
Are certainly in the way, no doubt about it
In Afghanistan we see that each man but fights today
In dust and dirt, mud and gore, hoping to find them
And settle the score. How many civilians lost, and who
Keeps that score? God alone?
To love one another as I have loved you, was Christ's
Heartfelt plea. (*Remember to be true*), and to his own
But hate alone does loudly roar, yet another roadside
Bomb, and yet more will die, and can you tell us *why?*

Margaret Lightbody

Parent

When someone has a child, I expect
A seismic shift;
An initiation,
Receiving the knowledge, becoming
Parent.

But there is
No transformation,
No metamorphosis; she
Remains herself.

More tired,
More responsible,
More needed,
More loved;

But still very much
Herself.

Katherine T Owen

The Old Lady

There she was again, that old lady,
As I passed by in my car.
I saw her in her garden then
Busy with weeds, and grass, and flowers
To take to church now and again.
Her white head bent, her feet splayed out,
And after, looking all about,
Then she stood, and looked up high
Thanking God for her piece of sky.

Sometimes I saw her by the gate,
Waiting for a ride to town
With anybody who would stay
A moment just for her to board.
She sat beside me all the way,
Chattering quickly, head from side to side,
Not missing anything on the ride.
And as we reached the old town square
She thanked me for the journey there.

But where is that old lady now?
The house looks quite deserted - lost.
Paint peeling from the window ledge,
At least a foot grown on the hedge.
The curtain net all grey and torn,
All neglected, garden full of weeds;
No flowers, except a rose's head
Bravely living in a bed.
I thought she'd gone - so someone said,
But then I heard that she was dead.

Catherine Bach

A Milestone

21 today! A reason to celebrate.
Well done, Forward Press,
Your achievement is great.

Many a would-be author
Has got into print,
By penning a poem
To Forward Press to submit.

The thrill of seeing one's work
Appearing in a book,
Friends and relatives
Are anxious to look.

It's a wonderful pastime,
The best way to express
What the writer feels,
While their views are still fresh.

Here's to the future,
May you go from strength to strength,
Many congratulations, Forward Press,
You truly are the best!

Joan Catherine Igesund

Train To Auschwitz

The clickety-click of wheels over rails,
the monotonous rhythm that dulls me to dream
as I struggle to breathe, crushed close to companions
whose clothes smell of dampness, whose breath makes me choke
while they wail and sob and mutter their prayers,
I think about Isaac and hope he will find me.

Torn from the ghetto, thrown into a truck,
I am being removed to where only God knows,
pecking my last crust of bread I remember
my mother singing sweet songs in our kitchen.
The man at my back swears and pushes me roughly,
I pray once again that Isaac will find me.

This cattle truck overloaded with suffering,
I see the old jeweller without his gold teeth,
there's the tailor who talks nothing but nonsense,
I wish I was home again back in the ghetto,
scrambling in ruins, hiding in shadows,
I beseech the Almighty to let Isaac find me.

The steam from the engine, the creak of the wagons,
the train brakes and screeches to final surrender.
Doors scrape open, fresh air gusts into my face,
shouts begin, there are blows and loud cries of pain,
they drive us as if we are slaughterhouse cattle
and I doubt if there's any chance Isaac will find me.

Bill Torrie Douglas

A Special Place Called Denbigh

Denbigh town, overlooked by the castle on the hill,
Built in the thirteenth century, a place of interest still.
Denbigh's fine walls were built at Edward 1st's behest,
Holding for nine months against Roundheads, so passing the test.

Born nearby the castle, a well known Denbigh son,
Henry Morton Stanley, renowned explorer, whose fame was hard won.
His finding of Livingstone, his main claim to fame,
In memoriam, a local hospital, proudly bears his name.

Robert Dudley, Earl of Leicester, left his mark on Denbigh town,
Granted the castle and lordship of Denbigh, from the crown.
In 1572 he built the library that overlooks the high street,
Becoming unpopular, the church bearing his name remains incomplete.

Denbigh, set among rolling hills and green fields,
Wild flowers in profusion, Mother Nature yields.
Denbigh moor, bleak yet beautiful, never the same,
The renowned Welsh sheep, surviving wind and rain.

Patricia Bannister

Stuck Between

What's meant to be
Will always happen
No matter what we do
We live our lives the best we can
What else can we do?
We hope and pray for a better world
So we can better our lives
But with wars and senseless bloodshed
We listen to all the lies
We had to attack, it was self-defence
There was nothing else we could have done
I guess the only speech they know now
Can be found in the bombs and guns
But for the innocent men and women
And children stuck between
A better life is out of the question
How helpless they must feel.

Margaret McGinty

Mumbles Pier

Hot sun, azure sky,
We tread the bare, baked boards,
As overhead kittiwakes wheel,
Protecting their hoards,
Their cries babyish and shrill,
Piercing like swords.

Below us the sea,
Mill pond calm,
Gently laps against the stanchions,
Barnacled houses,
Crustaceans' mansions.

Ragworm wriggling,
Are they aware of their fate?
To be put on a hook,
And used as bait.

Then we cast our line,
Out into the deep,
Hoping we get,
Some fish to keep.

Rod tip bends,
The line goes taut,
Dichroic gleaming,
Three mackerel we've caught.

Helen Miles

On The Right Track

The track sprawls and crawls through thick forest pine,
Adopted by no one, the council's or mine,
It steep incline leaves walkers panting,
A slip in the ditch leaves motorists ranting,
Stones tumble, waysides crumble,
Postman, milkman, deliver, then grumble,
Winter bites hard, a blanket of snow,
For seasoned country dwellers, is it really a blow?
A day off work with reason they say,
So sorry sir, I'm snowed in for the day,
From ice, a thaw, then H_2O,
Trickles to torrents where does it all go?
The muddy terrain mops up the wet mire,
For pedestrians alike it's gumboots attire,
Potholes of puddles form dark, murky pools,
Toddlers await disregarding the rules,
The sun come out and dries out the slurry,
Mud cracks appear tempting creatures to scurry,
A battlefield of nettles rear virulent heads,
By contrast, forget-me-nots, amass flower beds,
As the passage of time makes way to erode,
The transition is one of becoming a road!

Nicola Warren

Times Past And Present

Snuff
Mentholated memories of days gone by
Watering eyes
Frequent sneezing
Relieving breathing
And the misery of a stuffy nose
So I chose
A snuffy nose

Snuff
No need to smoke in harsh weather conditions
Nicotine addictions
Are satisfied
And pacified
By a tiny pinch of magic dust
So just be dedicated
To medicated
Snuff.

Ken Grimason

The Dawning

It's so easy to take *it* for granted - whatever *it* happens to be
For me today *it's* the sunrise over a calm north eastern sea;
The start of the day for the Farne Isles
In a silence to make the heart beat - when
Thousands and thousands of sea birds
Make this special occasion complete.

To think that it happens each dawning
When most of the world doesn't see
I am pleased *it* was just so this morning -
As I could pretend *it* was done - just for me.

No! I'll never take *it* for granted
We are here for a limited span - and
Must take each and every advantage
To absorb just as much as we can.

If by chance you can share such a moment
It's something you'll never forget - but
Should you fail to spare some time, and some effort
It will be something you live to regret.

Hazel Simpson

Joshua's First Try

Sure-footed he sped to score his first try
Strong, sweaty hands pressed from inside the maul
'Keep going, don't stop,' he heard his coach cry
The other team chasing, he wished he could fly
Ran fast as a cheetah, clutching the ball
Sure-footed he sped to score his first try
Faster and faster, legs pounding, sweat drips in his eye
Praying frantically, 'God, please don't let me fall'
'Keep going, don't stop,' he heard his coach cry
Onwards swiftly towards those posts so high
Fans chanting and cheering his name they did call
Sure-footed he sped to score his first try
Heart bursting, chest heaving, he thought he would die
He swerved and he dodged the opposition's big wall
'Keep going, don't stop,' he heard his coach cry
At last touch down, he heaved a huge sigh
As proud as a peacock, he stood ten feet tall
Sure-footed he sped to score his first try
'Keep going, don't stop,' he heard his coach cry.

Rosaline Jones

My Son

From the moment I felt you move inside me
I loved you
When you were born I marvelled at your
Perfect form
I loved you
The first time I touched your skin
All the love I carried for you within
Suddenly came to be
I knew I loved you

The years have gone by and I still marvel
At you
Your accomplishments, the way you have lived
Your life
Now, you start your own mysterious journey
With your own dreams and your soon-to-be wife
One day you will say, 'You are my son and I
Love you!'
Just as you are my son and, I love you.

Jo Stimpson

Out Of Sight

The small screws fall
To the bottom of the box
Out of sight
But they're still there

A family torn apart
Jobs lost, home gone
Who listens to their plight?
Does anyone care?

A bleak diagnosis
Though a drug might help, but
It's a postcode lottery fight
How can that be fair?

An innocent's cries
Go unnoticed, unheard
Offered no respite
Too late, we despair

Old and frail
Their pension just drawn
Then a thief takes flight
As onlookers stare

Don't bury your head
Don't look away
Keep humankind in your sight
And let 'good' win the dare!

Beverley R Stepney

Mountain Queen

My mind has thoughts of beautiful things,
Sweet singing birds with silvery wings,
Giant butterflies spreading their colours in flight,
Against a background sky of white.

And also while I think of these,
Visions appear of candyfloss trees,
Surrounded by hedgerows, gold and green,
Ascending to the Mountain Queen.

The steep mountain road is shining like glass,
And wild, pink horses feed on the grass
That's painted yellow here and there,
And green goats are watching without a care.

Black rabbits gather in playful fun,
While above, the rising purple sun
Shines above all that is to be seen,
In equal beauty to the Mountain Queen.

Yvonne-Marie Wiseman

November Beauty

Like woods and lanes my garden has
Put on November dress,
But, charming in its pardon, it
Gave me, I must confess,
A most delightful fragment of
Late autumn loveliness;
There was a sprig of ivy, and
Two roses, soft, tear-stained;
A tinted spray of sycamore -
Still dewy since it rained,
And small twigs with bright yellow leaves -
All that the lime retained,
Though humble was the offering
'Twas sweet when all seemed drear -
And proof that beauty's lurking
In the tired face of the year.

Greta Fraser Murray

I Miss The Avengers

Steed is the one for me;
M Appeal his sidekick,
Chelsea Mews and country lanes,
Vintage cars
And champagne.
A world surreal, but yet,
Mourned for real,
As times gone by;
Gentlemen and 'tie or die',
Immaculate pronunciation,
Suits that fit, in analogue action,
Gorgeous manners,
Super clothes,
Fabulous 60s,
Square, black toes,
Leather black,
Pine-studded walls,
No!
Like me,
Anyone who remembers,
Will definitely miss
The Avengers.

Sheila Livesey

Untitled

If sorry could turn back time
Mend the mistake
Take away the hurt
Repair the relationship
Convey the sentiment
Punish the regret
Reveal the remorse
Forgive the failure
Deliver the penance
And be
The warmth of a breath
The tenderness of a love
The strength of a soul
Then,
From the depths of my heart
I am sorry!

Fatima Z Ausat

Sea Birds Of The Southern Ocean

Skim, glide, rise and fall over the steel-grey, turbulent sea
In playful competition with others of your kind.
Wings stiff stretched you chase and turn in endless joyful swoop
Daring the waves to catch you with their spray.

Skim, glide, rise and fall over the heaving, mountainous sea,
Then silent hang atop the airwave in momentary rest.
For you, through night and day and sun and storm,
Must ever scour the freezing southern oceans.

The seascape of eternal raging is your challenge,
The twist of body, the control of flight, your laughing reply.

W Chapman

When Nobody's There

Look for the one who is lost in your heart and be ready
Ain't no one sure, with your eyes at the floor, that you're very unsteady

Alone, as the day starts to slide
The colours come into his eyes
No answers, but questions
Pass by, in disguise, no surprise then, when nobody's there

The newspaper's wet from the tears that he's wept, don't take it lightly
This limelight is shining alarming alone and it's blinding, so frightening

Alone in the backroom of time
He finds Cohen's words so sublime
As sure as he speaks them, he greets them and feed them, then needs them
When nobody's there

In treasuring words left behind
In painting a picture so fine
Inciting, igniting, inspiring
Then firing and riling when nobody's there

Alone, but his eyes start to shine
The image of you in his mind
The emperor looks so divine
In your clothes that he's wearing when nobody's there

Come here, go there
Watch how you hide
Behind the glass, there's no disguise
The minute you focus your blur, it'll worsen the moment you find nobody's there

He waits for the curtain to fall
The stormy waves stem that close call
He falls in the sea 'cause there's your love to drown in or frown in
And nobody's there.

David Palfreyman

Tomorrow

There is more to space than we think.
Much more. Much more.
Travel beyond the furthest star
and you'll find it's an open door
to infinity beyond.
Fantasy tries to describe
the world we will one day see.
Beyond the limitless space
of tomorrow, there yet will be
worlds to settle, to people;
to learn from mistakes of our own.
Worlds where high adventure
and the seeds of love will be sown.
We cannot even envisage
try as we may in our mind,
to think of the life that will flourish,
And the joys our race will find.
But it is all there - waiting -
while the stars in their courses sing
their shining song of tomorrow,
and the wonders deep space will bring.

Diana Morcom

Elongated Speech

I listen to music,
Where the beats sound out
One by one.
I flow with the rhythm
As my heart beats
With each melodious note.
My heart races as
My favourite song is being played.
I turn up the radio
So I can hear each
Note being defined.
Yes, I say
As the song concludes
And finishes with a
Perfect cadence.

I move from a place of
Solitude
To a reverie.
La rêverie. !El sueño!
The angels dance and
Prance,
Right before my eyes,
Right before my eyes!
Kissing and hugging themselves
And playing games.
I am in Heaven
As the music keeps playing.
I hold an angel's hand
And dance with it.
Then other angels
Join in, and we dance and
Dance.
Kissing ourselves and hugging
And dancing.

I open my eyes
And look around.

Yes, I say,
'If music be the food of love',
Let it play,
And play
And play on
And play
And . . .

Kumbi Johnson

Congratulations!

Congratulations! Forward Press.
You're twenty-one today.
May I wish you every great success.
In each and every way.
You choose to print the poems I write,
You select them with great choice.
You show extreme, within your team,
By using your inner voice.
I wish you many happy returns, on this special day,
May you long continue to publish the work,
On what authors have to say.
Twenty-one is the key of the door,
The key to great success.
Best wishes and happy birthday,
To all at Forward Press.

Catherine Fleming

Elegy For Isabella

(Who died 18th March, 2007)

Loveliest of dogs, you were the best,
You brought such comfort in your wake.
We feel the blessing you gave to each of us
When you leant against our legs and let us take
The silent benediction of your God
Into our being. You had an angel's touch;
When you moved and looked into our eyes
No words spoken could have said so much.

Your history was sad - a racing start
Which took its toll and left you a strained heart;
Northampton Greyhound Rescue took you into care,
A lady, searching, came and lo! You were a pair . . .
A mutual bond was born; she taught you how to live,
You taught her how to love and finally to give.

Rachel M Blundell

The Dream Maker

Making the dream suddenly comes alive and becomes real
A few chosen words put together with thought of mind
As a poet's pen soars, it drifts into depths with great zeal
Then comes out the other side as such fascinating prose

The vastness of wonderful words no boundaries create
Giving a window of possibility reaching out to mankind
Perhaps a world of our yesterdays for ours of today relate
A joy of reading in a quiet moment to one's heart's content

Dreams are the hopes when wished upon a moonbeam
Yet can fade with the morning dew like a tear on a pillow
Twenty-one years ago you gave the hope, it is clearly seen
For us to live the dream speaking through the art of words.

Dawn Prestwich

Growing Old Disgracefully

I will not pin my hair
Nor dress in black
Or sit alone in silence
Looking back

I will not show the world
A sombre mask
Or spend my time
Performing tedious tasks

Life's clock is ticking
On the mantle shelf
I want to spend my last years
Being myself

I want to swim a length
And ride a bike
To travel round the world
That's what I'd like

Don't wrap me in a shawl
And pat my hand
That was not the life
That I had planned

So brush my hair
And fetch my dancing shoes
The music plays
And there's no time to lose.

Patricia Kearney

Seventeen In Aberdeen

It's damp and grey on the River Spey
And it's dank and dark there too
But it's seventeen in Aberdeen
And the sky's an azure blue

How cold it feels in Gallashiels
And it's blowing quite a hoolie
But it's seventeen in Aberdeen
No need to wear a woolly!

The fog hangs thick in the town of Wick
And it's cloudy in Kirkaldy
But it's seventeen in Aberdeen
Where you can tan your body

It's lashing down in Lennoxtown
And it's drizzling in Dundee
But it's seventeen in Aberdeen
And it's the hottest place to be

The waves are tossin' in Ardrossan
And in the Firth of Tay
But it's seventeen in Aberdeen
And it's a very lovely day

There's a layer of mist in South Uist
It's below par in Stranraer
But it's seventeen in Aberdeen
And it's melting all the tar

It's a trifle dull on the Isle of Mull
There are showers up on Skye
But it's seventeen in Aberdeen
And nobody knows why

There's wind and sleet on Prince's Street
And in Stirling it's cyclonic
But it's seventeen in Aberdeen
And they're mixing a gin and tonic

There are winter storms in the high Cairngorms
And it's frosty in Carnoustie
But it's seventeen in Aberdeen
And it's just as warm as toastie

It's brass mon-keys around Dumfries

Snow's falling in Falkirk
But it's seventeen in Aberdeen
And they've taken the day off work

The sun don't shine in Kinkardine
Much less in Inverness
But it's seventeen in Aberdeen
Oh, yes, yes, yes, yes, yes!

The weather's poor in Stenhousemuir
And up on Arthur's Seat
But it's seventeen in Aberdeen
And they're dancing in bare feet

Few sunny spells on the Campsie Fells
Far far fewer in Forfar
But it's seventeen in Aberdeen
so shoen, so wunderbar!

It's extremely cool in Ullapool
And it's gloomy in Glenrothes
But it's seventeen in Aberdeen
And they're taking off their cloth-es

They've chilblained hands in Prestonpans
And it's vile in the Shetland Isles
But it's seventeen in Aberdeen
And all you can see is smiles

There's a belt of rain across Dunblane
And an air of trepidation
But it's seventeen in Aberdeen
And there's no precipitation

It's rough on the Clyde and in East Kilbride
And it's dire on the Mull of Kintyre
But it's seventeen in Aberdeen
What more could they desire?

There's no sign of sun in Livingston
And it's Spartan in Dumbarton
But it's seventeen in Aberdeen
And the celebration's startin'

The floods run deep in Cowdenbeath
Though shallower in Alloa
But it's seventeen in Aberdeen
With a warm Hawaiian halloa

There's a small typhoon blowing through Dunoon
There's a dearth of mirth in Perth
But it's seventeen in Aberdeen
And you can see it on Google Earth

There's some concern, today in Nairn
There's a hard gale in Ardgay
But it's seventeen in Aberdeen
That is all I have to say

Yes, it's seventeen in Aberdeen
And they're bursting into song
Aye, it's seventeen in Aberdeen
(But it will nay be for long!)

Rob Barratt

She Who Cannot Sleep

Though I may seem indifferent and holding back from life
Beneath the surface simmers such a torment and a strife
For someone has worked magic here, and someone's lit a flame
And my poor heart and soul will never, ever be the same.

To me, you are the strength of trees, the gentleness of flowers
The one who keeps me from my sleep, in dawn's soft early hours
So, should I die, or should we fight again and parted be
Remember, oh remember - that I once thought this of thee.

My joy, my love, my strength - my pain,
Adieu - until we meet again.

Diana Holmes

Close Togetherness

When we opened the pages of our people's history
We couldn't believe the misery
Of the old *Close Togetherness.*
Homes crushed together like books on shelves,
Streets groaning under the weight
And the people themselves
They had no room to notice.
Claustrophobia didn't exist.
Under the same heavy sky
Our ancestors all left for work at nine
And all came back at five.

When our forepeople broke away
They could never have known
That Scotland would become
Forever our homeland, never our home.
We don't visit these days
But try to keep the customs alive
By baking our bread short
And still we dance
To the skirl o' the bagpipes; old ways
Which may seem strange to our enlightened minds
But we've stayed faithful.

As a society we're civilised.
Our constitution bans war
Which it defines as angry words
Between two or more people. By prizing
The freedom to close any door wherever we are
We've put previous human conflict into perspective.
We are peace lovers and haven't lost
A drop of hostile sweat or blood.
Yesterday's *Close Togetherness*
Must have been such a strain.

Thérèse Stewart

Peter The Rock

He followed him at goodly distance,
Afraid to be recognised,
On this most dark and unjust night,
When destiny, justice had disguised.

He knew something momentous
Was about to happen this day,
That elements both dark and evil,
It seemed would have their way.

However, this day the universe,
Had a long time waited to see,
And before it is spent must peak,
Great and momentous destiny.

But he was mortal and made of dust,
His flesh could not withstand,
The things that Heaven had allowed.
Things he did not understand.

For at this moment in time,
His life was more his friend,
Than this claimant to immortality,
Who would not himself defend.

His mind had told him plainly
Of the dangers he would face,
But his heart beat him cruelly,
And his feelings he could not erase.

So while his master in the room above,
Like a lamb had nothing to say,
He below warmed his hands,
But himself would not display.

Then in innocence came a maid to say,
'Are you not one of them?
You look so anxious and afraid
For this man from Bethlehem.'

'I know nothing of what you say
For I am a stranger here,
I know not this man of whom you speak,
You have it wrong I fear.'

Yet another maiden came to say,
'I too saw you with him,
You followed him where e'er he went,
You are indeed his kin'.

'What are you saying, woman?
I never saw him before,
Neither yesterday nor today,
Nor do I want to evermore.'

Before another hour had passed,
The crowd came to insist,
'You *were* with this man, Jesus,
Why do you so resist?

A third time he cursed and swore
'Of him I do not know,'
And instantly as he was speaking
A second time the cock did crow.

They turned their heads and eyes enlocked,
And instant turned to hour,
As dizzying impact of words fulfilled,
Plundered him his power.

The pain so sharp within his breast,
The grief mixed with the tears,
His world ended at this point that night,
His soul forever seared.

The frozen moment worked well its will
As cosmic energy surged,
A new man was forged that night,
Peter the Rock had been purged.

R Blaxland

Music Spider

Spider-like fingers
Making love to the neck
Of the classic guitar
Turning out spine shivering melodies
As the audience sit breathless,
Drowned in a sea of notes and chords.

Climax after climax,
Crescendo on crescendo
Crash into motionless star-struck eyes;
All sorrows become forgotten memoirs
Written in endless tunnels of thinking minds.

It is raining music all around,
You hear the perfect sound
All spellbound to the bitter end
Absorbing talent from a newfound friend.

The night's echo's written in the stars
Like on a highway with speeding cars,
Sublime beauty of the music night
Change the dark into eternal light.

Werner Wehmeyer

Happy 21st Anniversary

21, 21, you have now come of age,
Where part-time poets used your publishing stage.
From across the country and the world too,
Your poetic family, it rapidly grew.
So congratulations and many thanks as well,
For giving us poets an outlet to tell.
Best wishes for the future and the next 21 years,
All at Forward press I now say, 'Three cheers!'

Anthony David Beardsley

An Epitaph For Displaced Trees

Permission was granted
to move an ancient woodland,
as if it were routine and possible.
They claimed tenderness in lifting stumps
to relocate these homelands.

The trees, however, need an epitaph,
nurtured within this woodland.
All around they lay like fallen soldiers,
slain beside their stumps and along the roadsides,
surrendering in thousands.

Fully uniformed against the summer,
stripped in the winter woodland,
or sporting toughened, needled snow gear,
root booted, and belted in bark,
fitted better than battalions,

a forest might destroy an army
enticed to fight within their woodland.
Instead, the ultimate in pacifists,
the trees gave centuries of sanctuary
and peace without conditions.

Wielding saws, a weather eye to profit,
they felled the ancient woodland
And the trees return in books, in winter warmth,
table tops - or coffins - from the massacre
in this abandoned wasteland.

Sue Cooper

The Countryside

Once we had the countryside,
As far as eye could see,
With woods and wild flowers,
And animals roaming free;
The silence was broken by birdsong,
Or wind blowing through tall trees;
There were cowslips and wild orchids,
Coloured butterflies and honeybees.

Then one day a farmer bought some land.

Now there was a world of fields,
Divided by hedge and gate,
With sheep that munched on cowslips
And cattle leaving grass in a state;
Machinery drowned out the songbirds,
And trees were felled to make room
For all of the crops to be planted,
Less space now for wild flowers to bloom.

Then one day the parish council bought some land.

Now there were parks and playing fields,
With all the grass mown short,
Most of the flowers soon disappeared,
All in the name of sport;
The birdsong was softer than voices,
And insects fled from the scene,
The ground was covered with litter,
The boundaries no longer green.

Then one day a business consortium bought some land.

Now there was a business park,
With buildings short and squat,
And tarmac roads and pavements wide,
Flowers in a concrete flowerpot;

No longer can we hear the birds,
Just the sound of cars and feet,
And the clang of the road sweeper
Sweeping litter off the streets.

When will it turn full circle
And revert back to its roots?
With the countryside we used to know,
Full of flora, fauna and fruits.
Perhaps we have lost forever
Our heritage of peace,
Of freedom to view nature . . .
Will destruction never cease?

Sarah Fernandes

Midnight Stars

Midnight stars dream of distant suns
And waiting worlds which glow and
Turn in silent hope towards
Our growing light.

A soft new song swells and ripples from
Our awakened heart, carrying sweet
Memories over cosmic seas
On ships of gold.

Silver sails catch spinning joy and lodestone
Points us safely home. Then the word
Is spoken from cherished thought
And we are there.

All before is beloved rainbow's misty shade
Dissolving, running, drifting . . . gone.
In *one* moment we live forever
Eternity is now!

Marian Gourlay Laing

Foreign Fields

Faces half buried in foreign earth
Blood seeps from every orifice
To match the oriflamme of bygone age
Teeth barred in ghastly grin
Death but moments away
The Reaper
Black robed
In raven wing
Pecks the field and takes his fill
Their glazed eyes may see him come
Or do their thoughts, on angel wing
Fly home?

Wendy Le Maitre

The Meaning Of Life

Where there is no hope, you despair,
Where are the answers to our existence?
Where can we find something that can inspire us?
Some people live blindly without cause or purpose,
They exist without belief or spiritual ambition,
They accept that life is imperfect and painful,
But do nothing to reason why our world is so violent,
Greed and corruption rule our everyday lives,
Yet we do nothing and allow wickedness to control our lives,
But our salvation is before our very eyes, yet we do not see,
Open your eyes and allow Jehovah/God to save you.

Alan Grech

A Saw It A' Sir

I'm neither a nobleman nor Prince Regent, Sir,
I'm merely a kinsman o King Robbie,
An a was on that field, Sir,
An I seen him, Sir,
Frae me tae you I saw him.
Plantagenets micht,
Their brave Langshanks, Edward himself,
Aye flayin his airms he fust an faught
Like an auld besom,
Aye like an old woman who had her plaid snatched
Frae her on a cauld winter's nicht.
Then he fled, Sir,
But he'll no be back as long as Robbie is King.
Aye freedom, Sir,
Freedom.

They a' fled, Sir, to the port o Airth
A'lang gan noo, Sir.
Their Dukes, in their fine splendour
Their breasts o yellow, red an gold, Sir.
O Yorkshire an Glouster,
All dressed in their finery.
Their steeds a'lyin in the mirth.
A joy to see them tak to their heels an run.
What a sicht, Sir,
What a sicht.
I seen it a'
A'lang gan noo,
A'lang gan noo, Sir.

Edmund Hamill

Green Blood

Just as the sap rises, forcing its rich greening,
Administering injections to every thirst-calling shoot and bud,
So is my heart hit by the rush of blood.
Burning with its life-giving oxygen and season beat.

Resurgence rising, my ancient emerald sword
Pierces the frost that coats and crackles, splinters and splits,
Fingers cold, old and calloused,
Gripping desperately to every root blade and death-soaked weed.

This is my wistful wish of coveting the Earth,
To experience the pervading new colour-tumbling and spinning
As converging winds gather, swirl and spread natural enchantment,
Interaction and exchange in the marketplace of sacredness.

Ever the fickle mistress, obsidian dark queen,
Old, new, dark and cold, turning distant and unknowable,
Seductively she spins and weaves each returning phase and receding tide,
She cannot leave us even when she hides.

I mark and check, wake, sleep and roll with the circle.
The wild spirit ever subtle and symbolic,
Full of potential, I enter, untamed yet honourable,
Tangled in the brambles of inspiration; wreathed in dark green mystery.
So as I bleed, so may I be,
In every stone and twisted tree.

Grant Howard

A Time For Reflection

It was cold I remember, dark too, and we shivered a little Did Ginger and me . . .
No time for a smoke, we were 'on guard' don't you see Guarding the camp . . .
just Ginger and me . . .
Our life-breaths spiralled upward from ice-cold lips; Genies out of bottles . . .
wraiths in the night

It was cold, you see . . . cold . . . and only Ginger and me.
'Til, of a sudden . . . we were *soldiers* we two . . . for
Someone was approaching from 'toward the town end'
Now . . . important, we challenged with a, *'Halt, who goes there?'*
Rifles were a-ready . . . our eyes burning bright . . . for we
Were the 'defence force' of Britain, that night.
No reply . . . no reply . . . we shouted again . . . *'Halt! Or we fire!'*
Still no reply . . .
The bolts of our rifles were drawn . . . and then returned, the clicks
Deadly ominous, startled the night - the answer came quickly
'It's *me* . . . it's *me* . . . I'm a *friend* . . . don't you see?'
And we saw in the starlight, a face pale with fright.
We 'advanced him to be recognised' - then with relief in our hearts
We said, 'Pass *friend* . . . *all's well'* . . . in the night . . .
And the civilian went by, on his way to his bed.
We had challenged the *'World'* . . . had Ginger and me - with
Five bullets apiece, but not one in the breech
We'd acted for Britain and freedom, that cold, starry night.
Yet, what was it for . . . that shout in the dark?
In daylight we'd have smiled a 'good day' and 'God bless'
But *war* is an aggressive creature in humanity's night;
Spawning hate, envy, fear and jealous offence . . .
Seeking to exploit and destroy, the affections of peace.

Gordon Reid Johns

Stepping Stones

When you created me 21 years ago
We had a long journey ahead
Unsure which way to go.
But my stepping stones in life
Have always guided me on my way
So thanks for 21 years
Life has had its ups and downs
But we have seen it through
So raise your glass as I propose this toast
Please don't ever change
Thanks for being you.

Pamela Page

Maiden Voyage

April is the cruellest month
As it was for the steel leviathan
On that fateful moonless night.

From the flat, still darkness
Looms a Goliath of growling glacial ice
Stark, menacing, foreboding.
The alarm is raised.
Too late to change course.

Ice eerily scraping, scouring, screeching against steel,
Piercing, rupturing, severing wrought iron rivets
Unceremoniously breaching
The structural integrity of the giant,
Freezing waters flow and flood
Forging forward into its bowels.

Consumed, overwhelmed, ravaged
Descending into the fathomless blackness.
A titanic battle lost.

Liam Heaney

Living On The Wire

My life is a circus,
A festival, a show,
An acrobat on a wire,
Rising high, plummeting low.

A gymnast, a performer,
Balancing a fine line,
Between heartache and euphoria,
In any split second of time.

A spectacle awaits those
Who venture to the edge,
Challenging the gods on high,
Unsteady, on a ledge.

So take me to the highest point,
Where anguish, joys and fears,
Push my emotions skyward,
To rapture, or to tears.

The higher that you climb,
The further you may fall.
But in the search for Heaven,
It's chancers that gain all!

Surviving on the wire
Is a true test of your worth.
Riding high one minute,
Before crashing back to Earth.

So climb down and feel secure,
Exist rather than live.
Or tremble on a knife's edge,
Experience all this life can give.

Never be afraid to tumble,
To really feel alive.
Life as a trapeze artist
Is the only way to thrive.

Mary Carroll

Who Am I?

I am stronger than I think I am
I am smarter than I know
I am more powerful than my mind leads me to think
I have a lot more soul-searching to go

I am kind when I am happy
But can be mean when I am mad
I am tearful for my family and friends
Whenever they are sad

I am fearful of my future
I am learning from my past
I am comfortable in the here and now
But not sure how long it will last

I am heading in my own direction
I am who I want to be
I am a person who respects herself
But above all I am me.

Shona Donovan

Above And Beyond

Too many memories crammed in one's mind
Good and bad all entwined
Thoughts and dreams you had and still have
Of having the family still around
To hear a knock at the door
Or ring on the phone
Could it be your sisters or brother
Or maybe your folks?
But this is a dream
That can never come true
Because in this life you know they've passed on
But you have your memories of those times past
The visits, trips, laughter with the family all there
Now when the clocks strike 12 at the end of the year
I, on my own, toast the family and say cheers.

Douglas Drummond

Fire Flame

Fire flame, I watch you dance
Your lapping tongues for me to trance.

Dreamy brow does wonder so
Orange heart and reddish glow.

Shadows cast long into the night
Stretch beyond and out of sight
Until only blackness.

Embers crackle, hiss, yes hiss
Oak burnt aroma, I want to kiss.

Smoke spirals puff and exhale
And your dance remains for me
To dream.

Andrew Russell

End Of Term

The business of abandoned school textbooks,
once industrious, churning out our histories and
Illuminating the mysteries of science
and religion and the fictional in-betweeners,
succumbs to a still classroom.

An unsteady line of graffiti-worn desks,
bellies not yet chiselled free from their forbidden gum,
coils around the room . . . but nothing moves,
nothing stirs, not even the row
of mysterious Aztec pots that ought to come to life
at night, or at weekends, or on holy days,
when no one's there to know.

Something was petrified by the alarm at the end of term.
Pupils were dilated; children scurried footlessly
through opened, half-opened doors,
taking their first steps into the summer break,
leaving the known world behind,
receiving sinister, more sinister,
more dangerous worlds ahead.

Mícheál Gallagher

Square Peg Syndrome

I phoned a helpline with a question to ask -
You'd think that would be a simple task;
But it didn't fit in with their FAQs
And that's when it became real bad news
FAQs are like pegs that are round
So mine was somewhat out of bounds

You ring a number, then hear a voice
That will tell you there's a multiple choice
Choose from these 5 options a voice will trill
But none of them quite fits your bill
So what to do now, choose one and hope?
Chances are you'll choose wrong and feel like a dope

What you really want is to speak to a human
Who'll treat you as an intelligent woman
Pressing hash and star is doing no good
You feel like banging your head on wood

Half an hour later, your senses are reeling
You're through to a call centre in Darjeeling
But the person there cannot help you -
The training is just for FAQs

So it's cost you a fortune, and all you've found
Helplines only work if the peg is round
So to get a solution just come out fighting
Use recorded delivery and put it in writing.

Margaret Campbell

Bubbles

Bubbles, bubbles
Everywhere
Shining all over the floor
Let's kick our feet
In the paddling pool
Behind the edge of the door
Let's hold on and never let go
As we bury our faces in leather
Singing songs we almost knew
Nothing to hurt us
Nothing to scare us
Nothing between is
As it should forever be
Shining amongst the bubbles.

Cyra Armstrong

Petals From A Balcony

A cloud of scarlet and crimson petals
Spill down from above,
Pirouetting delicately
As they clasp the breeze
In a silent, fluttering waltz.
Drips of colour stain sherbet-white snow
Blossoming chaotically
As the legion of scandal-red petals
Pour relentlessly down.
Flowers for the living.

Anneliese Paterson

A Moonlight Night

The moon lit up the October night,
I was once again a boy,
It showed to me the whole countryside,
Again I felt the joy.

I was back again at the top of the hill,
The top of the hill in our lane,
I look back at the white-washed house,
And still it looked the same.

'Tis a lovely night, this autumn night,
There's a touch of frost in the air,
I am a boy back home again,
At that home I stand and stare.

Alas, I must be dreaming though I am not asleep,
It's on the rocks, by the seaside I stand,
And gaze into the deep.

This moonlight night I think of our brother, Dom,
Who is sick and far away,
And if he were back at the top of the hill,
I wonder, would he stay?

Is it the moon that brings this on me?
Yet I am not in pain,
Though I stand on the rocks by the seaside,
I'm at the top of the hill in our lane.

Sometimes these memories, I curse them,
For they will not let me be,
It is the moon, it is the moon,
Or perhaps it's all just me.

Again I see that white-washed house,
Standing lonely in the bright moonlight,
For we are all gone,
There is no one there tonight.

Now I must grow up and go to bed,
And sleep that place out of my head,
Come tomorrow I'll walk by the sea,
And try to live in reality.

Paddy McCrory

Not Taken In

What assurance have you in your life?
Who are you going to believe?
Which of you has a cure for strife?
How to avoid thoughts that deceive?

Look at all the climate change news folks,
Do you believe it? Well, I don't,
Revelle of Harvard called it a hoax,
Maybe you worry, but I won't.

Revelle said it is a hoax he made,
And has told Mr Coleman that,
And this US weatherman has said
That truly we should smell a rat.

But, oh so gullible folk can be,
Revelle's hoax was for research cash,
Oh, open your eyes, open and see,
That there is this myth that we must smash,

And guess who was the enormous bore,
And Revelle's student at Harvard,
Whose film brings green taxes in store,
For all of us who are working hard -

Yes! You guessed it right, this is Al Gore,
Whose film, a litany of doom,
Is making waves on every shore,
Thrusts at you in your living room,

Making you feel guilty to drive now,
Guilty to even breathe indeed,
Causing hysterical folk to vow,
That Green Taxes are what we need.

So as you breathe out your CO_2,
With angered gasp, what will you do?
Will you seek that truth Coleman knew?
And tell MPs they haven't a clue?

Climate change is not the problem here,
But manipulation of truth,
Statistics doctored to make you fear,
A snare for fools and naïve youth.

So now's the time for us to speak up,
They will not force us from our car,
We'll not drink from their deceptive cup,
Let these words be read near and far!

Nigel Kirk Hanlin

The Beauty Of Siberia

A musk deer hind moves across the snowy wastes,
Where conifers and spruce grow,
But the cold is not to every species taste.

Arctic hares feed, play and box,
But they keep an eye out for a marauding wolf or fox,
And high in a nest, a bald eagle chick is driven out in a fight,
For food is scarce and to survive, one must use the law of might.

The Siberian wilderness is a beautiful showcase,
With the Biekal Lake and bears
And chipmunks roaming all over the place.

Patrick J Ryan

The Upper Reaches Of The Wye

Plynlimon crowned the northern sky
And owned the summer's glory
When to a bard the ardent Wye
Did thus relate her story.

I flow from freedom's central throne
And song, I love it dearly
As oft I sing in merriest tone
Where none but shepherds hear me.

Then through Trefaldwyn mile on mile
A southern course is taken
Through Curig's venerable pile
And Clochfaen Hall forsaken.

Trefaldwyn, as I pass from thee
I course a rock-bound alley
To where the Marteg brings to me
The streams of Garmon's valley.

Then, I would pause, if pause I could
When by that bridge descending
Where once old Castell Rhaiadr stood
The middle west defending.

Now Rhaiadr passed, I join the flow
Of Elan's minished waters
Which sings the song of long ago
The Nantgwyllt fairies taught her.

I gurgle on past hall and wood
And farms that are providing
Receiving Ithon's tribute flood
Two shires to be divided.

The Cammarch and the Irfon
Two rivers yet to mention
They join the Wye in Buallt Vale
It was nature's great intention.

But since that dark December morn
That closed Llewellyn's story
A traitor gave away the prince
Whose name is held in glory.

Then presently, through border dales
I glide a stately river
The lowland calls, but central Wales
I will forget thee, never.

R M Williams

Just Wishing

Most people like the sunshine, but I like the rain
And I'm always hoping I'll see you again
But if that doesn't happen then it wasn't meant to be
But I'll always wish that you were here with me
It is many years since I first saw you
Though how I felt you never knew
For you never spoke, you just passed me by
And I never spoke as I was too shy
Now when it is summer and we have sunshine
I still wish you could be mine
And in the winter when it is cold
It is hard for me to think that now we are old
And as the years go on and on
It is for you that I still long
Now as I walk alone, I wonder where you are
Do you live near or have you travelled far?
And when the phone rings I wish it could be you
For if it was, it would make my dream come true.

Eileen Kyte

On Barwhin Hill

On Barwhin Hill, a vibrant air
Spreads warm and gentle everywhere,
As from tall pine and yellow broom
Spills a fragrant, fresh perfume,
Whilst far below on a rocky shore
Lap dulcet waves in quiet encore.

Traverse then, Ardlochan's shore
As frothing waves of summer pour,
'Gainst craggy rocks of easy scale
Ascending t'wards a forest trail,
Thro' lofty trees, verdant and still
Amid the peace of Barwhin Hill.

Meander thus in true silence
Mid Nature's ferny ambience,
To reach pagoda's ruined fall
Where 'little monkeys' espied all,
In vista of a woodland pond
Tranquil-graced by gliding swan.

Stroll then by scented pathways new
Through shrubbery of brilliant hue,
To crested arch where thro' is found
A cobbled courtyard, circling round
Embattlements where mortar three
Sharp vigil keep o'er distant sea.

Perambulate green Fountain court
Where crystal waters skyward sport,
As marching band proudly displays
And lilting air serenely plays,
To West Green where in low redoubt
Sit iron cannon, solid, stout.

Beneath a pristine Castle keep
Of turret high and dungeon deep,
Standing proud in might and main
As tribute to baronial gain,
Staid domicile of quiet repose
But fortress once of stern purpose.

Thus, satisfied with tales of age
Retracing steps p'raps now engage,
O'er long cliff walk of lofty thrill
To reach again, quiet Barwhin Hill,
Thereon to rest in fashion true
And sunset beyond Arran view.

As with the world all proper seems
'Til by moonlight, Barwhin gleams,
Bringing time to slow descend
To shore below, and venture's end,
In pensive mood but homeward bound
As silence gathers, all around.

James Ross

Patsy

She's the height of a daisy aged only three
The pride of her family, Grandpapa and me
Her mum, dad and brothers wave her goodbye
Her first day at nursery school with a tear in their eye
She clambers onto the big, yellow bus
As she looks back thinking, *why all the fuss?*
I know I am travelling to a different place than you
With my big, enormous uniform and my backpack too
My attitude is big though my stature is small
I'm probably nearer a two-year-old, that's all
These people are lovely, they take me by the hand
Settle me on the bus, help me understand
Through time I will sit still, listen, settle down
Articulate all the things that in my heart abound
I have so many things to tell you
That in my head are stored away
Such wonderful celebrations in our house
When I can speak them out someday.

Pat Corry AKA Nanny Pat

PainPane

(The writer acknowledges the Crowned Bard of the 2002 National Eisteddfod (an established poet and playwright) as his inspiration for this poem. Not being fluent in Welsh, the present writer read the poem 'Awelon' in its English translation by John Norman Davies, Green Druid, who commented, 'The strange English, in parts, is because I have translated literally, keeping as true to the original as possible. Lines in italics derive directly from the original poem)

Pain is the whole of life.
What does not kill us gives us strength
To carry on our daily lives.
If words are windows on the world
And every word's a pane
And what we write is what we see,
Then our words become panes
Through which our world
Is shown to others.

These experiences that give us pain,
And we think first too great to bear,
With resolution can be used
With help of words to show the world,
Especially where like pains are borne.
That one survived - and so might you.
How good for others they can be,
If disseminated far and wide
Through panes of words.

Through the waiting room window
The Bard surveyed the painful world.
Recording all in Awelon.
Through pain and panes of words he shows
His father's pain felt through his own,
The troubles of the world in words
To help the sufferer through his pane.
Pain is the whole of life and yet
Again *pain is the whole of life.*

Some would deny all life is pain
And list a host of pleasures;
And further thought must then reveal
That there are different kinds of pain.
One is by thinking of the past.
As Madam Sera told the Bard,
You have a life in front of you -
A long life - now *go out to play.*
You need that also through the pane.

It is a momentary form
Of pain to think for but an hour.
Back to Canuting - King who's known
For sterile commands to the waves.
Or was this just a clever ploy
To demonstrate incompetence
Of fawning mindless courtiers
Who thought to please in such a way
But merely showed their emptiness?

Would a painless human life
Lack meaning for a human?
Would there be no development
In other than the body?
If we'd no chance to help our peers
Would life be without meaning?
I think the Bard has answered that.
He justifies his own career -
As well as his Awelon.

If language, written or spoken -
Can spread throughout the civil world,
Thoughts can influence far and wide
Through *the pane of every word,*
The non-lethal and healing gift
Can be of universal help -
One of the universal truths -
What doesn't kill the suff'rer gives
Curative power to one and all.

G D Lowden

Cherished Thoughts

I sit by my window, alone and still,
My heart near to breaking,
You see, I love him, Bill,
My life, my joy, my only one,
My dear heart, is gone,
Oh how, oh how can this pain be borne?

But hush, hear a whisper,
A murmuring sigh,
A beautiful presence is tenderly by,
A glimpse of my dear one, my own true love,
Softly, from the heavens above.

My heart starts to quiver, to flutter again,
Is this, I ask, not the final Amen?
A sweet peace enfolds me, a thought, so dear,
That perhaps, maybe, he is near.

Ann Monteith

Parting

Farewell my dear and needed friend
For I fear that we must part
As you will tread an unknown land
But I, a well-worn path

Days pass me by
But years stand still
And no longer will I pay
For all my deadly and worldly sins
That I plead guilty for

The curtain is raised and now reveals
A mental skeleton left behind
An emptiness, a shallowness
That leaves my mind a handcuffed bind.

Margaret Maciver

Butchery

We are cattle
We are meat
We are the victims
Of victory and defeat

We are bred to die
A miracle of birth
The mystery of life
Just laid to earth

We are at the killing fields

The slaughter house
Where horrors dine
We are carcasses
On a butchery line

Ripped and gutted
Chop, slice and hack
We are fresh or frozen
In battle flak

We are at the abattoir

We are cattle
We are meat
We are bottled feelings
And terror complete

We are packaged
We are processed
Labelled, despatched
Sinned and confessed

We are at the checkout

We are cattle
We are meat
Wrapped in a shroud
Covered by a sheet

We have served our purpose
What could be odder
We served our country
And became cannon fodder.

Stanley Conn

Realm Of Mists

She stands tall, majestic, towering on high,
Reaching forth to a flawless sky.
Bathed in bright moonlight,
Glistening winter white,
The mountain shines, in the dark of night.

Hidden secrets never told, of lovely maidens
And warriors bold.
Eager in springtime, fresh and green,
The mountain holds court
Like a stately queen.

Now in full bloom, a myriad of colours,
She watches over like a brooding mother.
Protecting in summer, those in her care,
The mountain is glowing,
New life in her air.

Cascading rivers tumbling down
Her slopes, now bronzed,
Golden, autumn-brown.
Leaping pink salmon eager to spawn,
The cycle of life in the mountain goes on.

Dark now, mysterious, trance-like almost,
Shrouded in mists and haunted by ghosts
Of past generations and seasons now gone,
Mourning the future of those still to come.
The mountain stands silent, but deep within,
Life is still stirring, a new age begins.

Katrina M Anderson

Extinguished

Sudden gust of wind mutters through the crack
Candle in the window sputters from the draft
Amber threads flicker trembling all about
Slender flames quiver nearly blown out.

Embers fitfully churn upon a twisted wick
Then darkness burns with a single lightning lick
A rising spark spit from a brightness now spent
A tendril of white smoke trails behind its vent.

Last drop of liquid wax spills off the edge
Trickles down the stick, below to the ledge
Gels in a pool opaque like a pearl
Windowpane soot stain black as a merle.

Air whistling inward sifts through shadowy space
Arabesque silhouettes contour a sleeper's face
Patterns on the walls of moonlit curtain lace
No sign now for the one out there who waits.

Isolde Nettles MacKay

The Big Wind

It was an inhospitable wind
That blew old people into hospital.
Woken tortoiseshell butterflies
Wished they hadn't and smallish
Hedgehogs rolled into a ball.

Scudding over the hilltops
Clouds soon became shrouds
As the wind added to the pain
Of young birds reeling from
The first blow of early season
Snow over Frenni Fawr.

Robert Wynn-Davies

The Middle East 2009

Can might impose right?
Should power play a game?
Rule justice and retribution the same.
Chase any cause, noble or base,
Mindless of the innocent?

Rockets fall from the sky.
Let them all die!
Missiles erase families.
No qualms, but homilies
Of clap-trap, saving face,
For sacrifice to the ravages
Of space-age savages.

She baked bread.
Her household was large.
This target was chosen
For no other reason
But to feed an obsession.
Deny the native's a patriot,
Let the invader expropriate
And crumble mud huts.
The west has gone nuts!

James Taylor

Tired Dogs

Tired dogs following
Tired owners
Wearily plod 'cross the grass
Evening's cool breeze
Begins to chill
Summer's not yet over
Autumn's begun to scent the air

The distant tide washes in
Unseen behind the dunes
A background sound

The last golfers
Well teed off
Longer shadows, from tee to green
Light fading slowly from the sky
Tea's been eaten
Evening TV news watched
Day's work done
Tired owners of tired dogs
Long shadows plodding across the grass.

Robert Stamp

When?

When is ecstasy a greening tree?
When is a drug a lily's scent?
When is happiness reflected clouds in the glitter-soaked sea?
When is yearning the thing you've waved goodbye to?
When is success the sunrise that also flames your heart?
When is life a flowing river?
When is joy - to you - the skylark's song?
When is dawn the open-hearted greeting?
When are stars the gateway to miracles
        - as they were in childhood?
When is bliss the backdrop to awareness?

When you come home to yourself . . .
        That's when.

Ann Palmer

You Read

You read books to pass the time
Every word and every line
Every phrase and paragraph
That make you weep and often laugh
Stories of fun and of true life
Of someone's up and coming strife
Words of wisdom, words of faith
Of human wrongs, and other race
You read of thoughts and harmony
Of long endurance and poetry
Of wicked lies, fun and games
Slander, slight and famous names
History of Earth, galaxies far
Children's fantasies, and fast cars
Everyday beings, and future hopes
Crime and murder, up and down slopes
You read for pleasure, never pain
To satisfy, to ease your strain
Looking forward to finding the crook
Life is like a never-ending book.

P Thomson

Little Chap

I am a happy little chappie
As little chappies go
In summer I play cricket
But I am awfully blooming slow
In winter I play football
I run and jump and fall
But everybody laughs at me
'Cause I never get the ball
In spring it's picking daisies
Bluebells, daffs and all
I take them home for Mummy
And she puts them in the hall
She puts them on a table
At the bottom of the stairs
Before I go to sleep at night
I have to say my prayers
God be very kind to me
Please don't let me fall
Or all my mummy's flowers
Will go flying down the hall
In autumn it's off with Daddy
Fishing rod in tow
I really don't like it
But he makes me blooming go
He says it's so relaxing
So sit down don't make a din
I turned to get my fishing rod
And that's when I fell in.

Aubrey Abram

A Beautiful Day

What a beautiful day
All sparkling and clean
Blue skies, green grass and flowers bursting

Farmers are out sowing their fields
Planting the seed
For the harvest to yield

Children are playing out in the sun
Running around
What a lot of fun

What a beautiful day
A beautiful day
What a beautiful day today.

Laura-Louise Thomas

Forward Press 21st Birthday Celebration

Congratulations Forward Press, you're 21 today,
The poets of Wales send their good wishes
Just to say . . .
Thank you for publishing our poetry
We have sent to you;
Some humorous, some sad, and some of
Human tragedies too!
One's experiences in life jotted down on a pad,
Perhaps sat up in bed
In the middle of the night,
We must be mad!
So, good luck and may God bless you all,
De-cork the champers and simply have a ball!

Margaret R Bevan

Chiaroscuro

The sky grew dark
As storm clouds gathered overhead
And, in a moment's chill,
A raven, harbinger of doom,
Alighted, wings outspread,
And murmurs of despair infused the trees.
But then a shaft
Of sunlight arrowed through a rift
Of gold and shimmerings,
Bright as a bluebird's wings,
Mellowed the breeze.
The past is history;
Tomorrow is a mystery,
The present of today's no gift
To squander ill at ease.

E Blacklaw

Rothie

The banks and braes of Rothie
Are really very bonny
The weather's dreich
And sometimes bleak
But it's still bonny Rothie.

There is a pretty roe deer
That visits, now and then, here
It stands nearby
Not very shy
And then there is no roe deer.

Catherine Blackett

Winter Landscape

It is almost the shortest day,
The sun sets at half-past three
Flaring in glorious saffron
Fading to palest egg-shell blue
At the outer edges.

The view from my window
Is like a Japanese painting:
Blazing satsuma sky a backdrop
To the black pagoda of the Scots pine,
To the grey hills sleeping.

Water flows between
Luminous pale grey chiffon
Reflecting streaks of flame
Fringed by filigree branches
Of silver birches.

So death should steal swiftly,
Blazing us to extinction
In a short sharp burst of fire;
Fading quickly in memories
Beautiful as mid-winter.

Lorna Ferguson Kirk

Lost For Words

I've a talent for writing: it's easy I said.
So I'll write you some poems ere I go to bed. But . . .

I sat up all night with pen poised in fingers,
I always use biro -
I find ink stain lingers.

I sank to the depths, my subconscious I stirred,
I enjoyed the experience
But did not write a word.

I soared to the heights with thoughts lofty and pure,
But how I should scan them
I just wasn't sure.

So I struggled with rhythm and metre and verse,
I used syntax and metaphor
And simile and worse,
Full rhyme and half rhyme and alliteration
Until in the end, the proliferation
Of all my ideas cankered my brain,
And I'll never,
    No never,
        Write
            Poetry
                Again.

Betty Westcott

Celebrations

There's many a true word spoken in jest
But I think it fair to say
Twenty-one years in the publishing trade
Deserves celebrating all the way.

Lift those banners, shout out loud
Hip, hip, hip hooray
Release the balloons, watch them go
Floating away with the soft breeze
That blows under the summer sun.

It's a lovely day to hold a joyous occasion
Thanks to Forward Press for being such
A fine institution
In giving budding poets the chance
To realise their goals
To put them centre stage with a much broader view
To help show off their creation
When given inspiration
Then to see their work finally appear
Set out in publication.

Now we raise our glasses in a toast
To celebrate this milestone being reached
Congratulations Forward Press
Long may you have continued success.

V Thompson

A New Life

She stands, a lonely figure
At the side of the sultry loch.
Arms aloft, eyes searching
For a lover gone . . .
A pale moon climbs the night sky
And a chill wind springs up
Whipping the surface into angry waves,
Hissing against the stones.
Her hair streams out damp and glorious,
Her cloak billows from her body
And her breasts stand proud,
Thrusting against her thin gown
Aching for her lover's touch . . .
Her cries are snatched then tossed away
As she sinks down
To lie at the water's edge.
Her hair in the water moves rhythmically
In time to the surge;
A sigh is borne on the wind,
My love, my love . . .
She places a hand on her belly and gasps
As she feels a flutter, faint and then again;
The sky is ablaze with stars
The moon now big and strong.
She rises and makes her way home
To wait for him . . .

Joanne Burns

September

With the sounds of laughter and voices
Penetrating a landscape so beautiful, but never remote.
From the trees, leaves burnt golden, fall
And flutter to the ground like butterflies.
Blackbirds fly in the soft grey sky
And sometimes, there is no sound
Except from children, trying to fly
Like the birds in the sky.
Water churns in the stony stream
And flows fast, almost like a multicoloured moving dream,
September's air is cooler, fresh and clean.
Perhaps an Indian summer is on the way?
On this bright, crisp, new, September day.

Christine Brooks Dobbie

Unemployed

What shall I do, Dad, now war has come our way?
Put on a uniform or stay this way,
With overall and spanner mending the old car,
Or go to the fight, Dad, and maybe win a gold star?

I've no money at hand, Dad, and no job to do,
At least in the army, they look after you,
So what will it be, Dad? You decide my fate,
I may even end up, Dad, by lying in state.

Thelma George

For Better Or For Worse

Have I been asking for too much?
For peace to enjoy ordinary things,
Gentle conversation with friends,
Quiet times for simple contemplation,
A film, a play, listening to music,
Simple pleasures others take for granted.
Going out and coming in freely
Without questions or recriminations.

Watching the marmalade cat lazily licking soft paws
In a shaft of sunlight on the window sill.
Hearing the lapping of waves on the sand
While leisurely strolling along a deserted shore.
Instead of these - harassment and grief -
Day after day silent suffering.
Dreading the key turning, constantly lying,
Covering the bruises, making excuses.

Yesterday though, Hope gave me strength,
Soothed my trampled spirit,
Told me it was time to move on
And, this time, no turning back.
I came here alone, wounded and weeping,
No bags packed, no time for possessions,
Desperate to reach sanctuary
In just the clothes I stood up in.

The faces of strangers here are kind,
Though etched with similar sadness.
Last night I slept a safe sleep
Wrapped in silky clouds of comfort.
But in the early morning light - a nightmare
Real and terrifying behind closed eyelids . . .
In one awful moment of disquiet
I thought I heard you calling.

A Caie

Our World

Oh! Maudlin world what is your story,
To free mankind for eternal glory,
Peace on Earth, is that what you see?
Peace on Earth, can it ever be?
For the end of wars, not the end of strife,
Conflict upon conflict throughout one's life,
Freedom to be free, the maxim for each and all,
But like the autumn leaf, the individual must fall.
Brainwashed on all sides with glib, subtle cant,
While the 'powers' lust for more as they cajole and rant.
And so 'our world' what more can we say?
Just hope for some future better day.
When all antagonists are united as one,
No killing, hatred, animosity or gun.
Or is there an enigma to be solved, or ever can,
That everything changes except 'Man'.

Dennis A Nicoll

I Know

Oh, scarecrow
Don't you know
I have no fear
For I have learned
That your ears do not hear
Your eyes do not see
And your hands
Cannot catch me
Oh, scarecrow
It is with gusto and glee
That I choose to sit on you
Rather than in the tree.

Liz Barclay

When Winter Turns To Spring Again

When winter turns to spring again, it casts a magic spell,
That strengthens with the lighter nights, and serves the season well.

Now buds on trees begin to show, in glade and woodland vale,
While daffodils in guard-like line, mark out a springtime trail.

In the fields, fresh lambs appear dressed in neat and woolly gown,
Helpless, cuddly - so serene, the sweetest, cutest kids in town!

Awakened waters spread to flow, through inlet, ghyll and glistening tarn,
Spinning on their downward ride another joyous, carefree yarn.

New hopes are raised - new life is born, and ever it shall remain,
Re-enacted on Earth's enduring stage, when winter turns to spring again.

Bill Jamieson

Friday's Phone Call

I magnified my sadnesses
On lonely shores; and hanging from
A silken thread, I trembled at
The thought of lives so prone to pain.
Yet somehow chance entanglements
Can fashion fragile webs of light
To bathe those inner darknesses
In pools of gentle absolution.

Distress can make us eloquent,
And call to those adjusted hearts
Where plaintiveness resides; and from
The self-same shores of memory,
Your voice across the evening waves
Arrests another dying day's decline.

Archie Gorman

Brave Swallows

Autumn's withered fingers pluck the air,
First leaves are down and bracken brown.
Their ocean journey, now prepare, brave swallows here,
Gone the latest brood, to follow sunlight, ready food.
Inside the church porch niche, their many nests affixed.
Swift swoop, they glide and swing,
Dear Lord, please bless their wings!
Blue-feathered fleet, vast ocean they must meet.
Life ends, the feeble one, be old or young.
And many never see the sun!
Warm Africa, the promised land to come,
Mirage - a dream, wave, crowding palms, where
English elms have been.
Like men, each bird awaits its fate, for
Some will die, without a mate.
Untidy, crumbling, need repair, their nests are empty!
Who to care?
Appear green blades, rejoice the heart of Man,
Since world began,
Watch first swallow skim the church again,
Repair its nest, where from an egg, it came.

A E Doney

I Heard A Robin

('Bonnie' our 19-year-old dog had to be put down)

I heard a robin singing o'er your grave;
Still in my aching heart there is a song:
Death shall no more destroy the peace I have;
A faithful God now bids that heart, 'Be strong!'

True comfort I shall find in loneliness;
Sweet memories return to cheer my day;
They shall remove from me all strain and stress,
And gladly I'll pursue my lonely way.

With youthful fervour you survived the years;
You brought me joy and so relieved my pain:
Now I at last can banish all my tears:
Find in my greatest loss the greatest gain!

All is not lost, I feel your gentle breath
When all alone I walk at eventide:
How strangely near, though in the arms of death!
Death, cruel death cannot true hearts divide.

Yes, there is hope, need I at last despair?
A loving God bids me from sorrow rise;
Too, like the robin I shall sing a prayer,
And guide my soul to God's sure paradise!

Frederick Crozier

Liam

Your boat was ready, Liam.
A gentle breeze played lightly in its sails.
We watched you go,
But couldn't follow.

Your little face, alight with love,
Your dark eyes, deep pools of childhood innocence:
The beauty of your short life
Helped fill the lonely places in our hearts.

We yearned to turn your boat around
And hold again the brightness of your smile.
But this was not to be.
Instead, dark clouds of pain and sorrow rolled between.

Then, angels came,
And the sky was filled with sunshine.
On wings of tenderness and pure joy
They bore you home to love itself.

Liam, we let you go
And know that one day,
We'll meet again,
In the glory of that other dawn.

Rose McQuaid

Davy's Friend

He came to our home every day,
Sometimes to eat, other times to play.
He ran around with the dog, stroked the cat,
And lay beside Davy to have a nap.
They played Snakes and Ladders, Snap and Donkey,
Then watched television after tea.
Tim came on picnics and trips to the beach,
He was never very far from reach.
Tim sent Davy to school,
They parted at the gate,
At the end of the day he would meet his mate.
When Davy was ill he sat by his bed,
Then when he got better Tim gently fled.
We never heard about Tim after this time,
The imaginary friend of this little son of mine.

Carol Rees

Looking To September

The days shorten, the wind blows
It seems as though the days of summer
Are long gone and the scent of the rose
Is only a memory.

Not that there was much summer
'Flaming June' was slow in coming
More rain than ever followed on
With tales of floods for evermore
The red-hot summer was a myth
And never happened.

It has been known
To come as late as September
There might be glorious autumn yet
We can but hope!

Elizabeth Love

Weather Permitting

Endless rain!
Each drop a thunder in my heart.
A reminder of things.
Clouding my judgement by
flooding my mind.
Dark sky - a sheet of sorrow
covering my world.
A glimpse of sun.
A blaze of light.
A rainbow of colour.
A change of mood.
A brighter future.
A ray of hope.
Another day.

P Grant

The Llanishen Scene

Ah! Llanishen your environmental status
Once reigned supreme
O'er wooded boundaries and farmlands green
Kindred enjoyed many a ramble
O'er your country scene
Your compound of nature held treasures galore
Flora, fauna, birds, insects.
An education for folk to explore
Summertime - kin walked to Cefn Onn Park
Starting at dawn, returning by dark
Folk admired your prize-winning station
As they waited for a train
Perhaps to Barry Island and back again
Scouts, Brownies or Girl Guides
Trekked along lanes and o'er hillsides
Children loved the thrill of
Camping, farms and the old mill
Paddling, fishing in your streams
Climbing, swinging from your trees
Families gathered blackberries, cobnuts on autumn days
At Christmas, cones, holly, acorns for Nativity displays
Aye! Llanishen, a different scene is on the verge
As the concrete and steel have begun to emerge.

Pam Ismail

Summer's Present

Should I embrace this summer's present?
Or should I let it be?
For this summer is but a fake
As unpredictable as the rolling sea!

The sea can be a gentle soul
And then a roaring beast!
The seasons too can change their faces
Just like that roaring beast!

These seasons they are a-changing
From east unto the west,
They spoil the season's outings
Like an uninvited guest.

I see the people of this world
Living under glass or
In some biospheres just like a hothouse plant
What will the planet look like then?
My mind is in a whirl, I'm glad I won't be around
When this world comes to an end.

Derek J Morgan

You

You weren't always wonderful
Understanding or just there
But the bond we shared
Was strong and true
There is a hole in my life
Now there's no you

I miss your smile
I miss your hugs
I miss your voice

We had some laughs
My memories are good
I try very hard not to brood
My life is good
My family well
I miss having you to tell

About my adventures
Both good and bad
About my days
Both happy and sad

I know others miss you
You were special to many
I wish I'd appreciated you more
And could visit you any
Time I wanted for a hug or a chat
I'd give anything for just that.

Rhoda Pullar

Skimming Stone

Soar free over cerulean sea,
across the ocean, meant to be.

Uncharted waters lay profound,
fuelled by mystery and lack of sound.

Visions and memories reminisce,
skin deep to grace a fleeting kiss.

Eternal notes on air unsung,
harmonies on the horizon. One.

A certain remnant of a distant heart,
born so fair and far apart.

Skimming stone, so few see true,
my tender heart,
my sacred view.

Matthew Beck

Suicide

In my nostrils the smell of
Yesterday's wreaths,
Discarded in a decaying heap
Against the cemetery wall.
My mouth fills with the
Bile of guilt because
I was blind and deaf
To your silent screams.
Could I have reached out,
Touched your life,
Stopped you?
I will never know.
Before I walk away
I gently drop a single rose
Into your open grave.

Patricia McKenna

Rabbie Burns

Rabbie Burns was born at Alloway, in seventeen fifty-nine
His family hard-working but poor
That was their lot in that time
Growing up a peasant, but with humour and fun
His writing expressing his values, attitudes to everyone
Yes, Rabbie, he was quite a lad
Liking the lassies, and some he made glad
But lots of others, he made sad
He wrote his poetry far into the night
His pen was busy by candlelight
First published in seventeen eighty-six
His poems were good, and quite a mix
A second edition of his poetry fine
Was published by Creech, a skinflint in his time
Burns carried on working hard for a living
To provide for his family, his wife loving and forgiving
Monies were few, but he wrote on
His talent was there, second to none
He died in seventeen ninety-six
A man in his prime, so much he was missed
His odes are now spread far and wide
Scottish folk toast him side by side
And now so famous that poetic man
His poetry is read throughout the land.

Sheila MacDonald

Without You

What is around me I know is there
Of the beauty of things I am unaware
There are no tears left they have all been cried
What shall I do? Where shall I go?
Without you, my love, I don't care or know
Life is now empty, without you I'm lost
A world full of sunshine is now full of frost
Our family try hard, I know that they do
Our daughter's inherited so much that was you
Our son is like me, cannot think what to say
But he tries very hard in his own special way
I sit here in this garden you tended with love
Feeling cold inside though the sun's up above
And hope soon I will join you in God's other world
For without you, dear husband, I'm no longer a wife.

Patricia Ann Davey

Spring In Rannoch

Surly, sullen skies shake squally showers
From steely clouds,
Sharp spikes of ice blot out
Hills and lochs with their
Temper tantrums.

Suddenly, sunshine spears the sulky sky,
Sweeping searchlights squeeze the clouds
To skim the Earth
With laser lights.
Creating calmness from chaos.

Maureen Reynolds

In The Bad Books

Once again I have entered the bad books,
Where most of the time I spend,
My bad points listed and dated with hooks
That pierce the skin but never the mind,
On the top line of every page,
The same word repeats like rain,
It is only spoken when she is in a rage,
That unflattering word, my other name,
Point one is my failure to wash the dishes,
Then there is forgetting to lift the kids,
Point three, not obeying any of her wishes,
Though I'd still be in the bad books even if I did!
For when my name gets scribbled down in ink,
I receive the silent treatment,
When those wedding day tears forced my eyes to blink,
I must have missed that small line of the agreement,
The book that always opens with a slam,
Captures every moment that is misunderstood,
The pen, the feeder of its taking hand,
Only tells of the badness, never my good.

Ian McNamara

A Memory Aid

There used to be a dance hall in Porthcawl
The name of which I tried to recall,
I would stand at the bus stop racking my brain
Looking at the gap, but all in vain.

Then one day when I was attending a class
I asked a member if he could remember
The name of the hall which I could not recall.

He pointed to my ring and patted me on the bottom,
I was annoyed at the time, but it prompted this rhyme,
So the name Golden Hind will now be etched on my mind
And very unlikely to be forgotten.

Rachel E Joyce

Baptism Hymn

We are gathered here today,
To help this little chap upon his way,
May he never see a hungry day,
And thus we break bread
To see he's not underfed,
We bless his soul,
We wet his head,
And may he reach three score years and ten,
And be a marvel amongst men,
His destiny is all wrapped up in you,
So may he live a life that's true,
See he gives his hand to hold,
Welcome soldier to the fold,
We can't give him myrrh, frankincense and gold,
But a faith which he can hold,
May he always walk in light,
And not in the forces of the night,
And now for this chap dressed in white,
Guide him along the road that's right.

Alan Pow

The Tall Ships - Belfast 2009

Where have you been
Since you last billowed into our lives?
Awakening pleasures previously unknown.
A swash of careless days, until,
Puffed up by a wind of conquest
You proudly sailed away
Leaving us beached:
Restless for the oceans beyond.

Yearning memories, in hold, for eighteen years
Surface on your return.
Dampened slightly by the years, yet,
We greet you pleasantly;
The ardour of our youth,
Scuttled now, by a younger generation.
As you leave in a Parade of Sail
We linger to wave farewell.

The tide of emotion calmer -
The ache has gone.
The ache has gone.

Margaret Cameron

I Remember Love

I look at each of you and I see my heart
I see all that has lived and loved in me
When I hear you laugh or see you smile
All the bright futures that I dreamed of are there
In your eyes and
I remember love
Often together we have talked long into the night
Afraid not of the dark
Nor what tomorrow may bring
Tho' each our own we are one
I the mother, each of you the son
Such times remind me of a little girl
In another world and
I remember love
The world moves on and in a future time
You will share thoughts with another
Such time will not be mine
And as you talk with pleasure of such joy
A shooting star reminds you of a little boy
You pause to ponder all there is above
And say aloud, 'Oh yes
I remember love.'

Sally Thompson

Loyalty

The sensuous softness of your touch
Is balm to my soul.
Solace when weary and dispirited,
        Seeking rejuvenation.

We have walked together, you and I,
For many a season now.
Our growing intimacy is exclusive,
        Unwitnessed.

You have no public persona.
You exist only within the seclusion
Of this safe, private haven,
        Alone with me.

Alas, time has not proved benign,
Insidiously creeping upon you,
Dulling the freshness of youth,
        To mellow autumn.

Perhaps we should part, you and I.
But, no, rejection would be too cruel.
You are so much part of my life,
My very own, my dear beloved, precious
        Bedroom slippers.

Alison Drever

Hope

Shall we mark our 21st with something rather grand?
A party, or perhaps a special band?
Let's rope in all our friends, so we will all remember,
And do something every month - right through to December.
Make a wish and see if it can come true,
Peace for everyone, and good health too.
Let us work together to make the future bright,
Don't give up, but instead join the fight.
Do you see many birds in our lovely countryside?
Is this a warning to help make it worldwide?
Can we make our 50th another celebration day,
To show how much difference we can make along the way?

J Miles

Belfast '78

Steel ball swings
        remorseless.
Mortared dust shrouds
        plastered remains
        and jagged brick.
Papered stripes exposed
        to bus weary gaze.
Secrets, birth, death
        invaded.
Depeopled.
Concreted windows.
Concreted doors
        Tenanted by skeetering
        rats,
        unafraid, multiplying.
The undefeated.

Rita F Marshall

Past Times

Maesteg by name . . . Fairfields to us
Once thrived with work, and thick black coal dust
Several pits, toiled tens of men
All happily grafting, they were then.

Remembering a summer day with Dad
A winding stroll, down a stony St John's Road
Enclosed by mountains, with hidden tales
Amid rolling fields and leafy lanes.

To see it now you'd never believe a colliery
Stood here with coal-rich seams
Gone are the wheels, the pithead baths
The miners' café, once a hive of chat.

No blackened faces, happy smiles
With wide, white eyes so full of pride
Gone are the days pit ponies run
Making the most of the holiday sun.

The miners' strike a long time gone
Left echoes of their tuneful songs
From mountaintop to our valley below
Their haunting steps they follow me home.

Ann Thomas

And Judas Came Too

Thirteen, they say, is unlucky for some
Twelve men at a table, plus one
They are all sitting, ready to dine
Their meagre meal, of bread and wine

Matthew, Mark, Luke and John
Peter and Andrew, all came along
To eat with Jesus, and hear him preach
The greatest miracle he would ever teach

Jesus bows his sacred head
Blesses the wine and breaks the bread
The bread and wine are now transformed
And the greatest miracle has been performed

Judas eats and Judas drinks
Judas sits and Judas thinks
Judas wonders if he is right
About what he must do tonight

Judas is uneasy, he knows the reason why
For thirty pieces of silver, Jesus must die
But his conscience makes his mind ask
Why he must perform this devious task

Jesus eats and Jesus drinks
Jesus sits and Jesus thinks
About tonight, when he'll be sent to die
He doesn't wonder, he knows the reason why

You know it had to happen
Jesus knows it too
If it hadn't been Judas
It might have been you.

John Tummon

How I Woke The Sleeping Plum Tree

It was really rather stupid
That tall Victoria tree
Year after year it blossomed
But not one plum for me.

I talked to it
They say that's good
But every autumn
It barren stood.

Last year I lost my temper
I kicked it with my boot
I shouted and I shook it
(I was really rather rude!)

Today I looked -
My heart it sang
From *every branch*
The green plums hang!

Claire M Wray

No Glorious Deliverance

Into station Bank Holiday serene
An age or theme needs no speed
Crazed dog of world all extreme
September black dry wet sweat
A gamble walking near a park
Or lonely from that final home
Eye whiskey and ravished stone
Bloom nettle soup leap so steep
Cold chill such climate says allowed
Hover so close that fainted cloud
Burst of spring and other days
A window or that imprint you know
Even without such usual snow
Her but then first lesson now
Stern lights a crossing red
Curious rage uncomfortable real.

Malachy Trainor

Nova

A soul that bleeds with need
While the evil around us breeds and feeds on whatever it likes.
It reaches into your life.
It takes what it wants, just for a laugh
And leaves a raw, gaping hole where there once was a heart.

Gill Hayes

Storm In A Teacup

Men! You don't know where you are with them.
They run cold, they run hot.
It's calm for a while,
But no sooner you turn,
He's at boiling point
And you're in hot water.
Steam is pouring from his ear holes,
Then he switches off.
Things start stewing and brewing.
Abuse is spouting out,
Bags under eyes,
You can no longer take the strain.
He's milking you for all you're worth.
You try to sweeten things over,
He's so strong, you're so weak.
The spoon stirs emotions,
Your head goes round and round,
There's a crashing sound,
The door slams!
It's peaceful now,
Time to sit down, relax,
And enjoy a nice cup of tea.

Mary E Hibbert

Watching The Stressed

Got myself fully into life's slow lane,
Finally got off the treadmill of pursuit and gain,
Life so much better now the stress has all gone,
Could no longer take that hassle,
No longer could take the pain.

Stopped getting worked up when the telephone rings,
Nothing to fret about anymore,
The pressure's all gone since I closed that door,
Now I just walk along and stroll and sing,
And I see better days and I do better things.

Have time now to watch others still taking that ride,
Careering around with no time to think,
Caught up in the maelstrom,
Swimming against the tide.
No time to appreciate life's smaller pleasures,
Money and materialism is all they seem to treasure.

So I lowered my sights and reduced my needs,
Don't want for much at all now, I'm easily pleased,
Thank God I had the wisdom to break free,
Make a lifestyle change that's suiting me,
Now I see fully the wood from the trees.

Still get a little flustered now and again though
When events come calling,
Got to tax the car, visit the hygienist,
Ran out of stamps, forgot someone's birthday,
Some least little things can just get a little galling.

It's a quirkiness that intrigues me,
That modern life should be easier with labour-
Saving devices and hi technology,
Yet the pace of life has quickened in such
A paradoxical way
So I chose to get off, loosened all buttons
And just live for the day,
Read books on how to cook
And study Indian philosophy.

Bernard Smith

Indiscriminate Love

In our day-to-day lives, as with others we deal,
And notice things about them, both imagined and real,
How easily and subtly can we discriminate,
As we apportion labels, or, to some class, designate.

Yes, with fickle human nature, it so often can show
Prejudice towards others, yet with God 'tis not so,
For He has no favourites, but, from Heaven above,
Loves *every one* of us with indiscriminate love.

No tarnished reputation, or failures of the past
Could make God forget you, or forsake as an outcast,
For, no matter where you've been sleeping, He gives truest rest
To all who, in faith, come to Christ and seek His forgiveness.

And whether you're well connected, in the best circles known,
Or haven't a single friend to truly call your own;
No matter who rejects you in your hour of need,
Your acceptance with God is fully guaranteed.

Your skin colour will not hinder, nor make you fall behind,
As God knows no apartheid, and is perfectly colour blind;
And your looks or appearance His compassion will ne'er dim -
All He longs for is faith's upward look to Him.

There's no refusal on grounds of age, disability
Or ill health with the God of equal opportunities;
For He spelt out your value, in red, at Calvary,
And all who come will, in Heaven, have then a perfect body.

And when you come to God, He never will ask
About your wealth or income, or your social class;
For, whether you have millions, or not a penny to your name,
The warmth of your welcome will be exactly the same.

No temperament, character or personality flaws
Could make God place on any an exclusion clause -
The scope of His invitation is an all-embracing one,
'Tis for the 'whosoever' and that excludes *none*.

And none could e'er measure the length, breadth, depth or height,
Or comprehend the wonder of the matchless love of Christ;
It is without any rival, and beyond betterment,
And you, too, may experience this love, Heaven-sent.

For, if you'll but come to the Saviour, and in Him believe,
He surely will accept you, and eternal life you'll receive;
He'll take you, remake you and fit for Heaven above,
As you prove His everlasting, unconditional love.

Ian Caughey

Practical Hay

Mr Acerbic wears a jagged smile.
Nurse Wetboard is sitting on his face.
Monkey-faced men leer in at the portico,
I am on the baby grand. Attack
Of the stranglers. We die
In misty, rosy dreams.
We die as we wanted to live:
Cowardly, elemental tinpackers!

Some days later I am still
Underneath the baby grand.
Mr McGonad is sipping his pint
Of corduroy. Mr Slipgirdle has
A firm. Nurse Rendition
Is throttling him with a noose.
Alibi is hammering in the windmill.
The electric is all blown away.

Paul Murphy

Dragon Dancer

I knew the beast was sneaky, but I didn't know how much
Until the doctor told me he'd left his ugly touch.
I'd always known he lurked about, waiting for a chance
But I still wasn't ready, when it came my turn to dance.

Wearing my best armour, I gave an anguished roar,
'Come in: don't loiter there, behind my lifeline door.
Sweep me round the dance floor, let me smell your breath,
Look me in the eye, brute, that threatens death.'

The music stopped; my lungs took flight, I was petrified
When up swept a dragon-king offering me a ride.
His fire warm; his claws unleashed, I felt safe on his back,
Now the table's turned, it's us on the attack.

We've spoken long and understand the enemy is cold,
We know he might be back, confident and bold.
My dragon makes no promises; no kindly words that heal
But he dances to a tune in which my fate is sealed.

Y H Farrell

Garden

The lingering scent of a perfumed rose,
Lilies moistened with dew,
Luscious green trees,
Whispering leaves, hedgerows sparkling anew,
Irises blooming in profusion,
Evergreen clematis entwined,
Radiantly displaying nature's beauty,
Gardener's paradise.

Eileen Brown

Bruar, April 2002

Listen to the birds converse
in flitting, high-branched
indifference to the human race.

They share not our sorrows, nor we theirs,
but they share our joys,
as we exult together
in the gush of spring.

Above age-carved rocks,
where down-leaping Bruar's river
rests calm in dark pools
before each further burst,
up-leaps the tree sap to the tree tips,
reaching up from Bruar
to the bluer skies of spring,
where, with each other,
amidst the *pointilliste* new leaves,
the birds converse.

Bill Symmers

Last Moments

The time has come for us to part,
You can no longer stay,
Although it truly breaks my heart,
There's nothing more to say.

We have enjoyed many happy years,
But we knew someday it would end,
So please wipe away your tears,
And hold me close my friend.

I see your eyes glaze over with pain,
And I know that the end is near,
If only I could find a way,
To take away your fear.

I try my best to comfort you,
But all to no avail,
Our favourite songs I sing to you,
But even these begin to fail.

I kiss your cheek as you whisper my name,
Then you give your last deep sigh,
You are at peace now, no more pain,
And so I say my last goodbye.

Marjorie Cripps

The Birthday

I used to love a birthday
With jellies, cakes and cream,
But now I'm getting older,
I really want to scream.

Those candles on the cake,
Their flames a pattern make,
They flicker, burn and hurt my eyes,
So many there - I'm sure it's lies!

I really don't feel older
And want each day the same,
Not celebration cakes 'alight'
And cream that spells my name.

Inside I'm still a little girl
With nipped in waist and skirts that swirl,
At parties then, I'd dance all night,
But parties now give me a fright.

Still, as I look around the crowd
And hear best wishes sung aloud,
I suddenly smile, noting their mistake,
They've missed two candles from my cake!

Janet Llewellyn

Newport 2009

Time warp strikes again
This year I was prepared
With television coverage of the moonwalk
Played for days
Black and white enhanced
Best footage recorded over long ago
So like what would happen in a sixties studio

Still it captured a spirit
All things are possible

And somehow
The anniversary mass for Sam Devenny
The first innocent to die
Prepared me too

When Hume, Durken and McGuinness
Left St Eugene's
To chat to relatives
I slipped away
As the girl of that past time might have done
A background figure to the march of history

'One small step for man . . .'

I am outside the holiday house
Of sixty-nine again
In the Newport street
And inside too
Glued to the black and white screen
On the cold range of a wet summer night
As Man walked on the moon
And pictures beamed to Earth
And there I am too
Reading in an upstairs room
As rain lashes outside
A book a day until the weather clears
Then
Johnny's boat on broad Clew Bay
Miraculous draughts of mackerel
Shared out upon the harbour wall
And
River fishing with my brother and Seamus

And dancing in the streets
Life in prequel
Full of vigour

Before I came this year
I'd retrieved that silver belt
With medallions of Apollo still on it

From the faux-bejewelled toffee tin
I'd used for trinkets then

And the ghosts spilled out
Those escalated northern troubles
Seamus in hospital after the accident
Strapped to a revolving bed
Knowing he'd never walk again

Yet each time I come
I feel the quick of life

'One small step . . .'

Somehow suspended promise
Still inhabits here

And I wonder do people grow to maturity at all
Or does gentle acceptance
Retain their life's spirit?

Ethna Johnston

Affinity

I have found a love
As rich as a pharaoh's tomb
I feel just like a butterfly
Emerging from its cocoon
I feel bold
I feel young
There is a song of joy in my heart
You're my charm of protection
When danger is near
You soothe away all thought of fear
I cannot breathe
I cannot think
My mind is in overload
We have risked a lot
To get this far
Our hearts sought each other out
A multicoloured destiny
Our paths of life marked out
Together forever
You and I
My one and only
Sweet Ally.

Donna Salisbury

Hallowe'en Night At Beacon House

It was Hallowe'en night in Beacon House
There wasn't a stir, but the sound of a mouse
As it scampered across the dance hall floor
Picking up scraps from the party before
Then from the kitchen came a hell of a clatter
It shivered me timbers and made my teeth chatter
So being the watchman on duty at Beacon
I thought for a minute the roof must be leaking
So up I did get and to the kitchen did go
And I couldn't believe the sight that I saw
For there was wee Wanda, the queen of all witches
Now what's that she's brewing? As I shook in my breeches
For with a little bit of this and a little bit of that
A couple of frogs' legs and the wings of a bat
Apple tarts left over from 12 months before
Fag ash and dust swept up from the floor
Everything went into this wonderful brew
Even tobacco that the old laddies chew
The stench it was putrid and poisoned the air
But it didn't annoy all the guests sitting there
There were banshees and goblins and Count Dracula at least
Along with some vampires he brought to the feast
They were lighting their sparklers, squibs, bangers and rockets
While eating Granny Smith apples and nuts from their pockets
Count Dracula then spied me when looking for blood
So I thought I should go as quick as I could
But his teeth flashed before me as I let out a scream
Then woke up with a start for it was only a dream.

J Shields

Mynydd Illtud

Dark clouds swirl
With menace
Round the mountain tops,
Spill down steep gullies
In the rocky scree below.

To the east the Sugar Loaf
Is blotted out
By sheeting rain that fills
The valley of the Usk
From rim to rim.

Here, bright shafts
Of sun set fire
To yellow tips of gorse
And silvered dewponds,
Steely-grey.

Heavily, the brown rolled bales
Of bracken lie
On sheep-cropped grass,
And here St Illtud lies, they say,
Beneath a mound of rock and turf.

Here Romans strode Sarn Helen
On to Brecon Gaer,
And many ancient tracks converge
At standing stone
And iron age fort.

Along this way the Normans came,
The great cathedral tower
A medieval cube
Of shadowed light,
Sunlit far away.

The sky darkens;
Marching through my head,
Behind the pattering of rain,
I hear the feet
Of long-departed dead.

Tim Raikes

Spring

Winter has passed, now it is spring,
God has put new life into everything;
He plans the season as the Earth spins round,
In the changing faces of nature joy is found.

The song of the birds awakens me each morn,
Gone are the dull days, dreary and forlorn;
The snowdrops and crocuses have raised their heads,
Glad to be out of their damp, wintry beds.

Now the farmer is ploughing his land,
Producing his crops with his hard-working hands;
At the farm the hens cackle and the roosters crow,
In the fields little lambs are skipping to and fro.

Softly fall the fresh April showers,
To water the crops, the trees, and the flowers;
Afterwards perhaps will appear in the sky,
A colourful rainbow where the birds fly high.

The glens of Antrim are a picturesque scene,
With waterfalls tumbling down deep ravines;
The scent of grass and trees fills the air,
And the bushes are aglow with berries rare.

Let's work at living like the busy bees,
We will bloom and fade like the flowers and trees;
But how radiant we'll look like the flowers in spring,
When around the throne of God we will sing.

Vera McNeill

No Sound

Imagine your life without music
Without the sweet song of the bird
Long days and nights filled with silence
Where not even laughter is heard.

No sound of rippling rivers
No sighing of leaves in the trees
No pattering sound of the raindrops
Imagine your life without these.

We don't only find God in a garden
We can find Him in every place
In the dew on the cobwebs at morning
In the smile on a sweet baby's face.

Now these we all take for granted
To these things we pay little heed
But if we can't hear this sweet music
Then life must be tuneless indeed.

Now the music of life is abundant
It swells all around and above
But the music that pulls at your heartstrings
Is the music of God's own sweet love.

Helen Carnwath

Sky Patterns Over Dyfed

I sit by the window of the plane,
Just two layers of glass between me
And eternity. The jet's big mouth
To my side, greedy for air, sucks,
Sucks and filters great streams of sky
Through its ever hungry mouth, shining
Smooth as silk, sliding its steel lips
Through dense clouds and out into the
Sunshine, far on the other side.

'Thirty thousand feet up, and a speed
Of five hundred miles an hour,' the pilot says,
As nose to glass, we view, far away,
The voluptuous curves of Carmarthen Bay,
And Caldey Isle, a jewel on a pendant.

I look below at the world falling away,
At fields and forests, rivers and lakes,
Planed into thin fingers of light and shade,
Mountains as small as molehills, all as patterns
Fitting into a jigsaw. We gulp and swallow
Our spittle in the pressurised cabin,
Feeling the power of riding the sky.
We are so high up, we see sky flowers
Cut from precision lines of ice, delicately,
Subtly traced on the panes of glass.

But this is a dead place now, above the passageways
Of birds, and all living things; familiar shapes
Below are too small to have any relevance.
As far as the eye can see, there is nothing
At all, but the naked sun, and that long
Straight line which divides the virgin white of
Cloud banks from the sky's vast everlasting blue.

Phyl Jones

Privileged Men Of Steel

We are the underprivileged men of steel
Cold, dank, stark, steamy world - for us anyway
Smells, noises, aromas, fumy world - for us anyway
All hours, hustle, bustle, never stops for us
We're always worse off than the rest - so we think
Middle of the night sensitivity, four to five-ish
But -
The ore piled, placid calm
Silhouette-shaped steel structures we see
Screaming, shrill, blasting, sudden blast furnace
Euclid massive trucks in their enormity rumble here
The underprivileged men of steel we are

Closeness of shift, camaraderie we have
Trusting, looking out, awareness of dangers
Life at risk - sometimes I suppose!
Team spirit saves our lives I know
The underprivileged men of steel - are we?

Glinting, golden, glimmering ores here
Mousing the landscape, enormity of ore
Around the world, similarities language no
Understanding similarities, abbreviated dialect
Around the world
The mills rumbling incessantly, mostly
Rumbling red rolling steel goes on
A wonderful sight for all it is
Then *crash*, cobbling steel, rolling no more
But minutes are lost, costly but soon
Rumbling red rolling steel goes on
The buzz from the industry we have
The underprivileged men of steel we are not
Experiences vast all over the world
It's the same for them as for us
They share the trials and tribulations
Ventures gained, ventures lost, it's the nature
The relentless industrial battle we're in
Common respect you can't take away
We're all winners you know

Rough, tough, smiling, joking men
Practical playing happy joking men of steel
With a serious special job to do
We all do it you know
We are - privileged men of steel.

Brian Lyons

Autumn

Harvest, home, fields' stubble bared,
Dotted black along the rows,
Scattered ranks of cawing crows,
Fallen grains, their bounty bequeaths,
Early morning mists in wreaths
Gossamer wheels spiders spun,
Designs revealed by the rising sun
Painted the seasons' colours bold
Aglow with russets, ambers, gold
No painter's brush can really capture
The canvas we see, the artist Nature
Time circles now, autumn beckons
Winds blow up to strip the trees
Swaying, bending, the onslaught quickens
Boys will gather the chestnut pickens
The leaves of brown fall with others.
Upon streets, the roofs, and into gutters
Blown about, whipped up then scattered,
The fallen leaves, the landscape's letters . . .

William Grant MacKenzie

You (Michael)

(RIP Michael Jackson)

You,
You are
The song
On the radio.
You are
The tap
Of every beat.
You,
You are
The dancer
Upon the stage.
You are
The fashion icon
Of magazines.
You,
You are
The voice
I will never forget.
You are
The music
Which fills the sky.
You,
You are
The rhythm, the music
And the beat.
You are
The face of
An angel.
You,
You are
The doves in flight.
You are
The King of Pop,
You never lost your crown.

You,
You are
The music that will never stop.
You,
You are
My
Inspiration.

C A Keohane

Memories

Who dwells on memories? Not I
Memories have gone by and by
Some are good, others bad
And some memories are even sad

To dwell on the past is the last resort
For people who live on gone by thoughts
They don't have a future only a past
And sometimes memories don't always last

So all you people live for today
And let most memories slip away
Treasure some good ones and some sad
But forget all memories that are bad

When you grow older and look back on your life
Remember only all the good times
And when you are older, you will want to recall
The most precious memories of them all.

Irene Joan Blair

Green As A Primary Colour?

Politicians all around the globe
Talk about 'green' as they enrobe
To fly to a conference - hot air to expound
About gases, con trails and waste underground
They don't visit our brothers - the chimps and the apes
Just dine on fine food, washed down with good grapes
Forests are cut and buildings erected
Our air gets worse as new towns are selected
To push back the jungles where Earth's primates live
(They are not greedy and they will forgive)
As their homeland is stolen and ruined for life
And we clever humans create yet more strife
For all living creatures who share planet Earth
Just how much desolation is profit worth?
'Walk to work - don't use the car'
The mantra of parliament as they sit very far
From the once green fields where wildlife roamed
Now covered with concrete and people are homed
Maybe less breeding by people is needed
And more thoughts of land which could be re-seeded
Global warming - possibly a cycle repeated?
As Earth gets older its defences depleted
Are we helping this third rock from the sun
By over populating and our need for fun?
Green is in the rainbow and part of nature's dress
So why change Earth's colours and cause such distress
To all the wild creatures and their habitats
When we have the power; 'Stop this change and alter all of that'?
Let's forget the politicians and their empty spleen
And use some common sense to keep our planet green!

Alan R Coughlin

Hallowe'en

Green, grassy, witches' hills,
Wind that wanders where it will,
Glowing eyes of phantom cat,
Red-rimmed eyes of demon bat,
Moon that shines upon it all,
Autumn leaves that softly fall,
Wild and eerie night all round,
Mist and screech and silent sound.

Sylph-like slipping through the fog,
Creeps the sly and sinful dog.
Shadows tremble, life's aquiver,
Fireflies gather near the river.
Dares a man to go abroad
Where the dusky night is Lord?
Witches, imps and goblins revel
At Hallowe'en so stalks the Devil.

Margaret Ward

What's In A Name?

Mumbai, Mumbai - a cosy sounding name
Sliding easily off the tongue like butter from a toasted teacake
But the bloody carnage the gunmen left that day in their wake
Better suited its erstwhile name Bombay
More criminal than cosy

Outrage, like fame, is fleeting and the world has moved along
Mumbai now resounds to Slumdog Millionaire
And Oscar nominations rare
While Indian children of face most fair
Get a glimpse of life in a Western lane
For them too life will never be the same
Does anyone really *care?*

Meg Gilholm

The Journey Home

I watched you climb the hill, your body weary
and pain in every step
Yet you were determined. Almost excited.
You stumbled and nearly fell, I could barely watch.
You struggled on so bravely, it almost broke my heart but
I was so proud of you, when you made it to the top
You turned just once and looked around
And took in every sight of the place, that you had belonged.
The colours of the hills and fields, the blue morning sky.
A wistful look on your tired face,
A lonely tear slipped from your eye.
I felt the touch of a loving kiss carried by the gentle winds.
I saw a light behind you, heard someone call your name,
You turned and walked
Out of sight
Over the hill
And you were gone.

They had gathered to meet you
And now it was almost time.
They had missed you more than you would ever know
Your family and your loved ones and good friends from the past
And then they saw you coming
Over the brow of the hill,
Tall, strong and handsome.
They were so proud of you, and you were coming home to them at last.
You were smiling when you saw them
And overcome with joy.
You looked round and took in every sight,
The serenity of this glorious place.
A whisper at his side, a gentle kiss
And he turned and took her hand,
The woman that he loved and time apart had changed nothing.
He loved her with all his heart
And hand in hand,
She led him to his Saviour, to the Lord.
He was truly home.

The clouds had gathered now beyond the hill,
A storm and heavy rain.
Someone was crying,
Their loss was Heaven's gain.

Caroline McKiverigan

Morgana

We will inherit that land of poppies, pomegranates
the bright isle which drowning men have seen
as the last darkness parts before their sight,
which rests, they say, beyond the furthest west,
but lies, in truth, beyond the stark horizon
at every compass point; to which the soul must turn,
quivering to stillness.

And while from that glittering sea we turn our eyes
it sends its signs to us: the hush
after birdsong in the dusk, the red sun
sinking beneath the Earth, and at the mass
looking from face to face, we see its light there,
as each sips the blood of the eternal kingdom.

Apples, and apple wine, brewed sharp and sweet
as the serpent's kiss, scents of cinnamon and clove
twine round the trees of those green glades
where we will meet again with those we loved,
and know them beautiful, as in their youth,
or in the hour when they were most themselves.

Edmund Cusick (deceased)

They Never Say

If your hands, in your pockets
Find solace and grace
You might as well have
'Lazy git'
Tattooed across your face.

Other 'lazy gits' will gather round you
Coz 'lazy gits' do 'lazy gits' attract
Loiter will you proudly
Whilst the workers wander by
Happy
In your Godforsaken pack.

With a blunt, rusty knife
You should cut off your head
For you've little but strife
To scrape up and spread
God help your wife
She's better off dead
Coz, if lazy in life
You're lazy . . . in bed.

All you do is kiss and tell
And live without a care
Wondering what to buy and sell
And squandering all that's spare
The Buddha teaches 'All bodes well'
For those who do their share
The Bible says 'You'll go to Hell'
I say . . . 'You're already there.'

All who gaze upon you
Make a judgement
It's instant . . .
And forever paves your way
But none will ever tell you
'You're a lazy piece of crap'
Because civility demands
They never say.

Mark Anthony Noble

Clouds

As I look up at the clouds in the sky
Lots of shapes form before my eye,
Big ones, small ones, some in between,
Faces of animals or people I've seen.
Elephants, tigers, ships in the sky,
Whales, trains and buildings fly by.
Clouds of cotton wool, a giant candyfloss
Making different shapes for all of us.
Imagination, you see what you want to see,
An ocean in the sky if you want it to be.
Clouds, they can tell you a story or more
Making lots of shapes for us to explore.
Lie on the ground and look up at the clouds
Forming images for you, shout them out loud!

Niall McManus

Retirement Contentment

In employment we worked
So hard to achieve
For future employers
We tried hard to please
Yes, we have gone through
Life's trials
And endured all the pain
So have risen above
To be proud of our aim
Hard tho' it seemed
We were blessed
With good health
Yes, this is the richest
A mountain of wealth.

Kathleen Mair

The Bonnie Hills Of Scotland

Come and see the Highland hills,
The bonnie hills of Scotland.
Sit by a burn and close your eyes - to visualise
The phantom sounds of a distant past, echo all around.
And sometime, somewhere, you will hear a lone piper
Stir your heart with a Scottish lament.

See the rugged hills and glens strewn with white
And purple heather -
And the rampant thistle ever near - Scotland's pride forever.
Come and watch the constant trickling clear water
Descend from the mountains on high
Then attend a ceildh -
A traditional Scottish music and dancing treat
To make your heart skip a beat.
And when your appetite has been fully whetted -
Of the sights and sounds of the Highlands -
Perhaps you will visit again
The bonnie hills of Scotland.

Agnes L W Berry

The River

There is a river that flows down from Calvary
And into the hearts of Man
Those who think nothing can change or make better
The blood of the Saviour can

As it flows past the hungry and dying
They reach out for the peace that it gives
Those who serve you by giving help to these people
Gain strength by the power that it gives

Lord, it flows through the world, nought can stop it
Tho' many will place doubts in our mind
Sure we have plenty of food and possessions
Who needs rivers of any kind?

But let it flow into your life and be different
Attitudes change be more a servant's place to retain
Let it flow service and love to your spirit
Be willing to let it flow free
When you do your life will be different
I know because it happened to me.

Edith Hillis

Damaged

Bruised, broken, hurt
But still defiant,
How can we forgive?
Or be humble enough
To say 'It's all right now'.
Only the love of God
For us, can make it real,
With love He said
We are forgiven.
So too we must forgive
With love, God's love
For us.

June Cooke

The Dividing Line

She, the great She Elephant of our tribe
From whom we had descended
Upon whom we had depended
Past her prime, and in decline, no longer defended
The ancestral lands' integrity and pride
But, rather, forfeited her authority
And their independence and identity
By vending them

The big field beside the house I was born in
Was split in two - a crude new boundary
Driven through
Artificial and incongruous; something unnatural
And amiss in our midst
Lacking the legitimacy of the hedges we'd been
Used to
Looking those lost acres within its wickedness
Excluding us forever

And then the hammer blows began
The base business of laying waste
That severed limb of land; its awful metamorphosis
A mockery of all that it had been
Like a garrison of some occupying power
A 'factory farm' for captive fowl called
'Battery hens'
The latest trend - caged creatures shut away
From the light of day and all airiness
An indecent heathen creed
A momument to Man's arrogance and greed

No, Gran, you could not have known
What it was that you began
And with your death and further land
Transference
The desecration has escalated, unabated
You would not recognise it now, at all
Elephant Man is at large, and loose across
The land

The trees and fields far receded
The farmyards extirpated
And, we, the last left of our native line
The dispossessed and disunified
An enfeebled, spayed species.

Kevin Woods

Mama

O Mama dear, I loved you so
But I know I had to let you go
Pain took over
And I stood back
That's the day my world went black.

I can still see your smiling face
And your arms open wide
To feel your touch
And your gentle love
Can only be a gift from above.

Mama, I don't feel frightened now
Because you made me strong
You said, 'Keep going and chin up
You'll get along.'

Well Mama dear, you were right
People hurt and put me down
But I'll move on
Without a fight.

Mama, I love you
And I miss you so
But I see you always
Especially when I feel low.

Thank you, Mama, for being you.

Joan Craig

Disunion (Reunion)

Have you ever wondered why
You suddenly feel that inward sigh?
Well it happened like that for me
When at the bus stop I came to see
A boy I'd been to school with back then,
We must have been about nine or ten,
There was still that same boyish grin
Though now there were hairs upon his chin.
He said, 'I've meant to give you a bell.'
Then his words upon me fell.
'I've arranged our class to meet.
Maybe a glass with something to eat.
I've booked a room somewhere local,
Somewhere quiet, not too vocal.'
We arranged to meet the following week
While through me crept a cowardly streak,
How did I come to agree to this?
I'd just been given the Judas kiss.
Well, the time came to face the throng,
After all, what could go wrong?
The faces seemed to be a blur,
Unfortunately, my words took on a slur.
I decided to dive straight for the bar
But really hadn't got too far
When two voices behind me I heard,
I know you'll think this too absurd.
'Is that . . . you know who?'
'Remember, her with holes in her shoe?'
'Hang on I'll give her a call.'
'Hmm! She seems to look so small.'
Before I could move another inch
I felt their deadly, evil pinch,
Trapped like a fly in a spider's web,
I felt my courage from me ebb.
'Fancy seeing you,' I heard myself say,
'I'm not too sure I'm going to stay.'
'Relax, you're amongst friends,
It's time yet before the evening ends.
We want to know everything,' the one purred.
Once again, my vision blurred,

Before I could even move a muscle
To a corner, they proceeded to hustle.
'We couldn't believe our eyes,
Oh, don't get us wrong, it's not your size.
Naturally, you've grown a shade since then,
It's a long time since you've seen a *ten*.'
'Don't be a bitch,' the other said,
'You'll be putting ideas in her head.'
'Let's get onto a lighter note -
Remember that navy overcoat,
The one you wore to the trip,
Its hem held up with a paper clip?'
I stood there, certainly not through choice
When through the battle there came a voice.
'Time's up ladies,' it loudly said
Then to the bar my boyfriend led.

Leonora Brooks

Removal Day

The van has gone, the house is cold and still,
I feel an urge to close the door and fly.
Yet I am drawn to look again at familiar features
Though there is strangeness in seeing corners,
Free for the first time from screening cabinet.
Faded patches on wallpaper, where stood the chest
And long, long before that, it seems, the toy cupboard.

Thirty years have gone since we moved here,
Years that of late have been of such short measure.
When we came, with children young, and one not yet at school
The place was loud and brash, with tears and laughter mixed;
Never quiet, never orderly, but always full of life.
Now, all is still, the children grown and gone their ways,
Living their own memories, creating their own faded patches.

Robert Mortimer

Ocean Deep Blue

Door number fifteen stood defiantly
brooding under a half-moon glass
blazing wild-eyed livid blue.
Chunky brass fittings,
smoke glass panels,
solid and unwieldy.
Just another portal
fronting a tiny walled garden
on a uniform street
yet one which laid claim to me,
evoking sorrowful fields
of crushing regret.
It was a sleeping mad dog
lying patiently in wait:
launching itself,
all slaver and fang;
snapping at my heels,
snarling at my wheels.
An inebriated yob
loitering behind the acacia:
lurching into the street
jeering and taunting,
swinging at my head
with a bicycle chain.
A smouldering blue ire
nursing wounded pride:
holding on for both of us,
cradling the loss;
forcing me to remember
what I longed to forget.
I tried alternate routes,
went out of my way,
but I was spellbound,
magnetically drawn;
hopelessly lured
by its siren call.

It was all that was left:
a death knell,
a tombstone,
hallowed ground.
Then one day, finally
they painted it grey,
and I passed by unnoticed.

Robert Burden

Contra-Attraction

I cannot fathom sense from it;
This plethora of contradictory hints
Confuses me and I wonder whether you can fit
The scattered jigsaw pieces which make me wince?
Why did our teenage years coincide?
Why did our reactions differ in such a drastic way?
Dissimilar flotsam thrown up by the tide,
One stranded, the other reclaimed another day?
Is the undertow too strong for our control?
Are we helpless victims of the storm,
Neither certain of our allotted role,
Disagreeing what should constitute 'the norm'?
Why 'deep affection', that much each of us own:
You overwhelm me, yet I am not your type?
Only Eve was Adam's 'flesh and bone from bone'.
We are not separated by propagandist hype.

Morris Catherwood

I've Put A Heart Attack In The Sandwich For You

I've put a heart attack in the
Sandwich for you. I know that you're
Normally feeling quite peckish
By now. So eat it up and burp
It down as it settles in your
Thoughts. I know you enjoy the hunt
For your food when it comes and like
To talk over a long conquered
Meal. So eat up for tomorrow
You can eat up another heart
Attack, but perhaps, this time you
Can add a bit more relish. The
Morning knife layered it thick on
The bread, the thing you have got to
Remember, is that heart attacks
Spread real easily and there it
Is sitting on the full of the
Plate ready for you to eat. Yum!
Fear not, there is plenty more where
That came from and there's more bread
In the fridge. So help yourself as and
When but don't make a mess on the
Stone floor again. By the way, I've
Put a heart attack in your fresh
Sandwich for tomorrow to take
To work. And if you wake up in
The middle of the night, you could
Eat one then if you'd really like?

Terry Endacott

Valentine

I've loved you for a long time
But couldn't let you know
'Cause I belong to someone else
And know it can't be so
But every time I see you
I die a little more
I know there's someone wears your rings
And it's her you're living for.

You held me once within your arms
Your lips sought out for mine
And once upon a long ago
You were my Valentine.

The years have changed our lives a lot
It's good most of the time
But I'd give the world, if for just today
You'd be my Valentine.

Josephine Graystone

My Garden

Will anyone know I've been here,
In many years from now?
Will there be anything to show
The things I did, and how
I walked in the garden, tended the flowers,
And loved the roses on the bowers?

If sometimes I come back to visit,
Will anyone suddenly sense my spirit,
And know that I was happy here,
In the garden which I hold so dear?

There's a secret place at the bottom,
Between the roses and fir trees,
Where I sit, all else forgotten
In the sun, and hear the soft breeze.

If anyone, in the years to come
Is aware of someone they can't see,
Someone walking beside them
In my garden, it might be me.

Georgia Jones

Just Dreaming

If I could 'fly' above the clouds
To see the world from such great height,
Would I then 'see' the vast crowds
As 'He' does, from His throne so bright?
And would I 'find' where Heaven is,
While flying through the starry night?

If I could 'swim' through all the seas
And meet the creatures of the deep,
Would I then 'hear' all the pleas
From those who mourn and those who weep?
And would I 'find' the treasures there
Left from shipwrecks, for Man to share?

If I could 'run' o'er all the lands
Up the hills and through the dales,
Would I find the shifting sands
Along the shores, from here to Wales?
And would I 'find' the mountain high
For me to climb up to the sky?

If only I could do these things
Then I'd be happy with my dreams,
For I would need a pair of wings
And a set of fine, strong 'fins'.
Thus to ask the last request
'Good legs' and 'feet' to run their best.

Sylvia Clayton

The Vision

An angel came to see me,
He took me for a walk,
We followed halls and corridors
And then he stopped to talk.

He whispered in his silken voice,
The love God had for me,
Then signalled with his finger,
The way to go and see.

I crept into a silent room
Where love hung all around,
Words of peace and glory spoke
But never made a sound.

Arms tightly bound me to him
Yet I couldn't see a thing,
I only had to feel the joy
I knew his love would bring.

A warm glow took my senses
To a far and distant place,
My body drifted off into
The realms of inner space.

I heard the pain of children small,
Their bellies underfed,
I felt the sorrow in the wail
Of widows as they bled.

I tasted fire in killing bombs,
The scorched and battered land,
I smelt the blood of dying men,
Their tombs of shifting sand.

I saw the floods,
The fires,
The death.

An angel came to see me,
He took me for a walk,
He led me to the people
And left me there to talk.

Lin Freeman

Café Rendezvous

Lady in black with doleful face,
With coiffure of jet precisely in place,
Eating and drinking at ladylike pace,
What are you thinking, my dear?

Are you pondering spending tonight alone,
Without him for company, all on your own,
Despite the attractions you've carefully sown:
Is this the prospect you fear?

Or are you immersed in thoughts so sweet,
Of memories of times when you and he meet,
Of being embraced and swept off your feet
With passion and love so clear?

Lady in black, impeccably dressed,
So all who see you are duly impressed,
Relax and rejoice, do not be so stressed,
Look up . . . at the door . . . he is here!

Raymond Holley

My Beloved Friend

Come alive my love
And live your life.
Open your eyes
And take my hand
My beloved friend
Come into the light
And dance upon the sea
No tears will fall
Beneath your feet
Arise my love
My fair one
My beloved friend.

B G Ryan

The Days Of The Serviette

Oh for the days of the serviette
Of polished silver on tables set
Happy guests come down to dine
Out on the prom, by half-past nine

Punch and Judy are on the beach
Where Bible punchers, your souls beseech
In the arena the brass bands play
'This is another lovely day'

Hazy mountains over the bay
Gave promise of a perfect day
Persistent anglers digging the bait
While seagulls stand and patiently wait

Donkeys plodding along the shore
To them it seemed an endless bore
Candyfloss and bucket and spade
Children's days of these were made

See the side show, fun at the fair
With gay abandon, never a care
On the big dipper, hear the girls squeal
Or ride sedately on the Ferris wheel

After lunch we thought we were free
Yet they all rushed back for afternoon tea
Ice cream and popcorn and cockles galore
How did they find room for anything more?

The old clock tower is ticking still
As the setting sun dips below the hill
Shrimp boats arrow a crimson sea
Into magic moments of artistry

A concert party is in full swing
From far away, hear their laughter ring
Couples dance at the end of the pier
While bosom pals swill pints of beer

The carnival queen catches everyone's eye
As six white ponies draw her by
And in late summer on August nights
The town was a beacon of coloured lights

These are the things that I recall
Of those pre-war days, when I was small
And though I've travelled far away
My heart is ever in Morecambe Bay.

Peter Lob

The Vanquished Are The Victors

Now the battle is over and no one really won
The war that we are fighting has only just begun
Politicians have sent us here to help this country's plight
The more I see of this, I wonder if they are right
For me the fight is over, and I'm dying in the poppy fields
                              of this barren land
My blood is staining patterns on the dirty sand
I will no longer see my family or hold my baby's hand
They will glibly call me a hero, but I don't think that is so
We are merely pawns in their game of war and this they truly know.

Peter Merrin

In Memory Of The Battle Of Britain

Come, my lad and sit by my side
And I will tell you a story,
About this land and its pride,
Of England and her glory.

Not many years ago, my son,
Not many years ago,
This land was threatened by the Hun,
A great and mighty foe.

We were not prepared for war
In those sad, far-off days,
For war came to our very door,
We seemed as in a daze.

The hours were filled with sirens wailing,
No rest by day or night,
Bombs came whistling, children crying
In shelters, shivering with fright.

A call to arms was sent to me,
To fight for what was right,
Upon a ship across the sea,
We fought with all our might.

The enemy thought this land would crumble
'Neath the weight of bombs and guns,
But with a grin and many a grumble,
We won the war fought by her sons.

For bloody were the battles fought,
In the sky and land and sea,
And great was the destruction wrought,
What was to be must be.

Midst blood and sweat they fought each day,
To win for us our freedom,
Never must we forget the way
We kept our English kingdom.

Dear God, please grant, that never more
However far they roam,
No foe shall land on Britain's shore
On this our English home.

R F Caulfield

Flowers Are So Beautiful Any time

Flowers are so beautiful any time
When someone is well or when someone is dying
Or when someone is down and feels like crying
Flowers are so beautiful any time

Flowers are so beautiful on display
When someone is departing or going away
Flowers are so beautiful any time

January, February, March, April, May, June or July
Or any time of the day
Flowers are so beautiful any time

August, September, October, November, December
Flowers are something we should always remember
Flowers are so beautiful any time.

Sally Pinnock

Sonnet V

Since I must leave, let me bid you goodnight.
Love, lie you still and waken not for me;
For when the morning sunrise comes to light
I'll creep away, ensure you cannot see
That sorrow gives me eloquence to cry
A wealth of tears, though they be simply dumb;
I should not touch you, whispering goodbye,
With tongue pain-tied, lest I again succumb.
Since we must part, better it should be so,
To leave you with my dream upon your smile;
And softly I will walk away and go
Into sweet pain's oblivion for a while.
Since I must leave, let me leave you sleeping
And spare you pain of looking on my weeping.

Fiona Fraser-Thomson

Whispers Of Love

With just one meeting
We were strangers no more.
It was not just a friendship
It was love for evermore.

How I remember
Days gone by.
Things which happen
To make you laugh or cry.

Let me remember the good days
With a smile upon my face.
Thinking of treasured memories
Your wonderful, beautiful face.

How precious a memory
Entrusted solely to me.
A love to last forever
For eternity.

I cherished all you gave me
From day to day.
With your whispers of love
Locked safely away.

An angel came from Heaven
Taking you away,
Leaving my heart
Feeling sorrow and pain.

Love lies sleeping
I'm dreaming of thee,
Making it special
A treasured memory.

A smell so divine - it fills the air
Perfume so strong, beyond compare.
It's heaven-sent
And I know you are there.

Music of two voices
Of heartbeats - loud and fast.
A sigh, a breath, my silent love
In all the world, I still love you best.

How beautiful a memory
As I'm dreaming of thee.
Love itself shall slumber
Until eternity.

Margaret J Franklin

The Busker Plays

In the high street
Near a poster of a well-known band
The dancing tune as outside star land plays on

Children stop falling into musical reverie
Adults generally walk on calling young ones hurried to move on
Some slow down their pace, to pass little ones' coins to aim into hat
An angry person goes by saying aloud, 'Poor excuse for begging'
As the music plays on at the outside concert with no name

Many are good, many are not
Most most likely trying
Some will go on to enjoy golden days if lucky enough to be entered
                                              for the eligible raffle

Others will settle for silver and bronze
While others will settle for the pleasure of making music
And the highly skilled unprofessionally playing lover of music
The frustration of watching the majority of 'Top of the Pops'.

Miles Burman (deceased)

A Christmas Story

Please, dear Father Christmas,
Wrote the small child with her pen,
I would like a farmyard
With a goat, a pig and hen
And perhaps, if you could spare her,
A pretty little doll
That I could dress and comb her hair
I'd call her Little Moll.

Her writing she had finished,
Laying the note beside her bed,
She clambered in, the night was cold,
The pillow soft beneath her head,
Now deep within her dreamland
In came Dad with feathered tread,
He took the note that lay there,
One soft kiss upon her head.

Then, downstairs to Mother,
Who sat there with a frown,
He looked at her with sorrow,
Then quietly sat down.
He laid the note before her,
Already he had read,
The room was filled with silence,
No words need there be said.

'Oh, Dad,' said Mother sadly,
'What is there to be done?
Savings, hardly any
And such a paltry sum.'
Father watched her tears fall,
His heart was filled with pain,
He prayed within, with all his strength,
This scene, he'd never see again.

Then with love he took her hand,
To quell her wretchedness,
You *will* have everything you wish for,
Her wishes will be blessed.
Next morning, bright and early,
He dressed, then made his way
To a rendezvous in secret,

To a town where secrets lay.
Weeks later, it was Christmas Day,
Snow lay all about,
Was joy to see the faces,
Hear happy children shout.
The child had woken early
And there in the dim light,
Was everything she'd asked for,
Santa came at dead of night.

Father heard her laughter,
Then looked at Mother's face,
He closed his eyes with thankfulness,
With time he'd won his race.
'You are so good,' said Mother,
On his shoulder, laid her head,
'Now we have a Christmas
Without a fear or dread.'

'My love,' said Dad,
'In all this world
I live for just one thing,
To touch you both with happiness
From sadness, take the sting.'
That day was just like dream time,
Full of laughter, bright and gay,
With peace that lasts forever
That would never fade away.

Night was now upon them,
The child to slumber gone,
A smile still on her happy face,
A smile to linger on.
In the quiet firelight glow,
He sat with joy inside
As Mother stood beside him,
Her heart so full of pride.

One last embrace, then up the stairs
He went with silent tread,
Remembering much about this day
As he laid his weary head.
Downstairs she turned
Contented now, noticed something unforeseen,
What's that, a space upon the shelf,

Where Dad's precious watch had been.

A ticket, there, upon the floor,
She read, then realised,
A receipt for fifteen pounds it read,
Tears filled her weary eyes.
And that's how simple love can be,
Just think beyond oneself,
Remember, the happiness it brings
And that space upon the shelf.

Peter Ayers

Don't Blame Him For Everything

Where was he during my time of need?
When I prayed for succour he paid no heed.
When hope has waned on our knees we fall,
We recourse to him, last of all.

In the name of God countless are slain,
As Man sacks and plunders his earthly domain.
The bomb, the bullet, the gun and the knife
Take a terrible toll on human life.

Starvation, retaliation, will such evil ever cease?
Will the nations of the world ever live in peace?
The sceptics among us may say 'I know best,
There is no God, I'm an atheist.'

If people would only do what's right,
There would be no reason to hate or fight.
If folk treat one another with good intent,
God's love will find us in the end.

Catherine (Rena) Soloman

Timeless

During our lifespan, we all yearn to belong
Yet we are just one in a mighty throng
We are born belonging to our kith and kin
Then our youth when we dance and sing
For many years, we work and play
We belonged, succeeded, earned our pay
Well done, great guns we were praised
A feeling of comfort our spirits raised
Cheered on by colleagues and jolly fellows
Alas pride of belonging with age mellows
Family, associates, move on some long gone
A new chapter opens, but life must go on
Like Alice in Wonderland we sometimes feel confused
Join a Mad Hatter tea party and be amused
Show others who feel lost they still belong
With goodness and kindness help them along
Belonging is timeless as years pass we say goodbye
Each generation see just how quick time flies
When our days end and we are here no more
We will have timeless belonging on another shore.

Kathleen Fry

Blue Skies And Butterflies

Oh, those lovely days of blue skies
I thank God for those wonderful things
When the rain clouds are so shy
And the bee decides not to sting
As I watch the beautiful butterfly
I can hear the birds sing
And then I sigh
I wish God had given me wings

As I sit in my garden alone
Amazed at all the colourful flowers
I feel like a queen on a throne
Could sit here for hours and hours
I think to myself, *I'm not alone*
As I watch the spiders with their powers
I'm glad they made this their home
As I while away the hours.

Nechell Walker

Borrowed Time

If I should walk on barren land -
Heart, heavy as a stone -
Though I could see for miles and miles,
I would not be alone.

For you would be there, by my side,
You'd make my spirit soar -
Afford me strength to journey on,
So I may face the world once more.

I'd feel you there, where I would walk -
Your breath upon my face,
No voice I'd hear, tho' I would see,
The footprints that you trace.

For in that moment, shared with you,
My heart would feel no pain,
I'd linger there, in borrowed time,
'Til you must leave me once again.

Patricia A Mathieson

Parents

To have kind and loving parents
Is a joy beyond compare
They will always want to help you
And assure you that they care

They share your tears and laughter
And many a tear they shed alone
But the things they do the best of all
Are the ones you have never known

The prayers and the sacrifices
They offer up on your behalf
So that life may treat you kindly
And they will be able to see you laugh

In return they ask for nothing
But their wish must surely be
That they have sown enough of seeds
For your path in life to see.

Teresa Bell

The Road Of Life

(For my grandchildren)

The road of life should be filled with joy
For each little girl and each little boy.
First lesson we learn should be right from wrong
Then we grow up with a heart that is strong.

Walk tall, be proud, and hold your head high
Be honest, be kind, don't ever lie.
Help your friends along life's way
Do a good deed every day.

The road may be tough and people unfair
It won't always be easy to show you care.
A smiling face can light up the sky
But don't be ashamed when you need to cry.

Remember always to say your prayers
For there's someone up there who really cares.

Patricia Long

The Essence Of Love

That kiss of tenderness,
That removes all of my sorrows,
Helps me stand up tall,
And face all of my tomorrows.

That hunger in my soul,
That makes me want you more,
Even those welcoming arms,
As I open that door.

The truth in your eyes,
As they meet mine,
And this Heaven in my hands,
Which makes this love so divine.

I hear sweet music playing,
And I know, I love you.
I hear birds singing,
And I know, I love you, too.

So whether it be the rustle of the breeze,
Or the rivers flowing,
The sun setting,
Or, the flowers growing,

I guess, I don't want to lose you,
For you're more precious than my being.
For my life has changed completely,
And I cannot believe what I am seeing.

Your heart is beating inside of me,
It's there, both day and night,
And I'd search to the ends of the Earth for you,
If you were not in my sight.

Are your eyes seeing like mine,
How beautiful the world really is?
Is your heart singing out loud,
When we both kiss?

Falling in love is only
The very, very beginning,
But the true essence of love
Is when two hearts start singing.

So forget the hurt of the past,
And leave go of all your sorrows.
And stand up tall, my love,
And look forward to your tomorrows.

Time is not on our side,
Our life is ticking by,
And I want to spend my life with you,
So in your arms I'll die.

Yes, God created a pathway
Of life for us, forever,
So hand in hand, in harmony,
We can live our lives together.

You are more lovely than summer,
For you're very special to me,
And you're more beautiful than the sound
Of the surf down by the sea.

So no more hurt, no more tears,
No more sadness, and no more pain.
Just tears of joy, and sounds of laughter,
And this time, no more rain.

Linda Jennings

Song Of Sandness

As the Bard walked by Annan
He sang of its praise,
And the green woods of Nithsdale
He extolled them in lays.
But I bide in Sandness
Where there's scarce a green tree,
So I sing of the things
Which are so dear to me.
The wild waves, the sunsets,
The bright Northern Light,
The rainbows, da hömin,
The swans in their flight.

He sang of the mavis,
The blackbird and thrush
As he saw them and heard them
On many a bush.
He sang of the daisy,
The moose and the plough,
He sang of the inn,
And the sheep on the knowe.
But I bide in Sandness
And close to the sea,
So I sing of the things
Which are so dear to me.
I sing of the headland,
The geos and the seals,
The stacks and the skerries,
The boats and the creels.

He sang of the maidens
Of Mauchline and Ayr;
The weemin and ladies
He lo'ed them fu' sair;
He sang of the lassies
Highland Mary and Jean,
He praised all their virtues
As if each were a queen.
But I bide in Sandness,
And it's quite plain to see
I must sing of the folk
That are sae dear to me.

For there's true hearts and beauty,
None Sandness surpasses,
So drink up a toast
To our island's own lassies.

Stella Shepherd

A Walk In The Woods

Bright sun a-beaming
Green leaves are gleaming
Brown paths a-winding
O'er dappled gold
And misty blue

Glad birds are singing
Sweet scents are winging
Warm hearts are thrilling
O'er orchids rare
And sweet woodruff true

Happy feet are walking
Merry tongues are talking
Watchful eyes are seeing
Our bluebell wood
All fresh and new

And as joyfully we wend
Our footsteps home to go
Our thoughts will oft to bend
To the woods where bluebells grow.

Hilda Gould

Celebration

If I could stroke the velvet flank of the black panther,
What a memory to savour,
What a story to tell.
If I could meet a tiger on his travels and say,
'Hello fine Tiger, how are you?'
If I could fly to Antarctica to visit the penguins,
Would they trumpet a welcome?
Shuffle round, to make a space for me?
If I could hear the pounding feet of the cheetah,
Listen to the blue whale's haunting song,
Or hold the tiny sculptured hand of the racoon;
And oh, if I should meet the kind giraffe,
I'd thank him for sharing my world.

I imagine these things sitting in my chair,
Hugging myself in awed delight.
But if I could stroke the velvet flank of the black panther,
And she in turn, may introduce her young,
Then, that would indeed be a memory to savour,
A story to tell.

Alma Shearer

Fit Is't A' Aboot?

Fit on earth's it a' aboot?
Ye're jist as puzzled as me nae doot,
Fit wye shid Jimmy hae TB
Fin a'thing's gan sae weel for me?
Fit wye shid Acky brak an airm?
He disna deserve tae come tae hairm,
He's a better man than me bi far,
Bit life for him could scarce be waar.
His Quinie dee'd fin she wis five,
A'mfower score noo an still alive,
His wife's MS an in a cheer,
Canna walk, an gweed behere,
She wid niver hairm a flea,
So fit wye's she ere instead o me?
Fit wye div I hae a I need,
An yet the warl's sae fou o greed
That thoosans canna get nae maet,
They canna e'en get owt tae aet?
Mountains o food o ivry kine,
Some o't rottin' we ken at fine,
Fit wye kin we nae get it ere,
Far folks are deein in despair?
Fit wye? I could go on a day,
Bit man I dinna hae a say.
The warl's eneuch for a'body's need,
An plenty spare - bit for Man's greed,
The warl's a richt - a bonny place,
It's fowks ats lackin - short o grace,
Ivry morn daylicht braks throu,
Anither gran like day for you,
Coont yer blessins - look aroon,
Naething ere tae warrant a froon,
A smile - a kin' wird disna cost,
Tae start the day an naething's lost,
Spik tae a'body, miss oot neen,
Tae life's en ye'll nae lack a freen.
Fit on earth's it a aboot,
Maist o's dinna care a hoot!

Peter Nicol

223

Change

Bombs no longer falling out of the sky
As Field Marshall Keitel fixed a monocle in his eye
It is twenty-three fifteen on the eighth of May
A date now known in history as VE Day

The surrender now complete on this day in forty-five
There is much celebrating for those still alive
We owe it to the memory of those no longer here
That they will inspire us to a future without fear

In the fifties there were ballads and the start of rock 'n' roll
There was Jerry Lee and Elvis as well as Nat King Cole
This was the generation who made a lot of noise
With their flashy suits and hairstyles came the teddy boys

In the sixties there was Dylan and 'The Times They Were
                                  A-changing'
But as time raced on it could have done with rearranging
The flower people had ideals and wanted to be free
But their ideas on love and drugs were not as they should be

A pop group known as a nation's fab four
Had the girls all screaming and crying for more
Known as The Beatles, their fame was worldwide
With The Stones and The Who, Britain's music was her pride

But little did we know we would lose our urge to sing
With the murders of the Kennedys and Martin Luther King
Marilyn Munroe, John Lennon and Elvis also dead
Those who seemed so full of life now in their final bed

People die of hunger and also drug abuse
With AIDs and the homeless, some ask, what's the use?
Mankind reaches for the stars and walks upon the moon
With promises of better days *we all hope* will be soon

We now live in an age of videos and computers
But life isn't easier for travelling commuters
Everyone, it seems, just has to go by car
It doesn't really matter if they aren't going far

If only we could see humanity succeed
In changing this world of envy and greed
There are far too many people wanting even more
Forgetting the poor on whom they shut life's door

Going back to VE Day when freedom was achieved
I wonder if the dead would ever have believed
What the future held and how it would unfold?
Would they approve if they could be told?

Stanley Brown

Aestival

Ceanothus pungent bee-buzz blue
Entwined with golden honeysuckle fragrant,
Cavorting high summer wind dance
Scenting waves overflowing garden.

High on roof tiles sparrows chirrup,
Roses trellis-crawl pink perfumed blooms,
Sun seared earth-dun crumbles anew
As beans plump and swell under shady stems.

Sweaty compost mulches sludge-brown,
New apple-marbles form on leaf strewn boughs,
Promising plums burgeon bowing branches,
Empty snail shells signal thrush's feast.

Distant throbbing engine grumbles
Mowing weekly fast grown lawns,
Nettles waist-high, sheep a-munching,
Scarlet poppy-flashes amidst ripening corn.

High on warm airborne thermals
Buzzards wheel and stretch the sky,
Skylarks sing flying higher and higher
As lazy summer sun floats by.

Rosemary England

The Shores Of Loch Assynt

Leaving the house I wander
And wonder where to head
This cold March day when being inside
Yet again, is almost trapping me.
I need to wake and walk.

Green mossy path with snow slipping
March wind dropping off
In the lee of the ruin, I catch
That familiar first spring sound -
Two oystercatchers trilling by the loch
And know why I came.

Now ahead a little bridge
Built just for me
And, of course, the few summer visitors
Drawn to castle ruins, sunsets over the water,
The falls, or just the peaceful isle.
Here the track leads to shingly beach
Where yellow-ten stones crunching comfortably,
Hear wavelets lapping the edge, clear and fresh.

The Calda ruin is surprisingly tall:
A past-people shelter now fading,
Campsite yet for future travellers, while
Charred logs in hollows persist.

Toward the castle, find safe ground paved by recent hands,
To reach the sandy causeway, where the welcome sound and sight
Of those industrious birds is unmistakable: grey and white
Black bands and low-lying shapes, beaks poke the stones -
Yes plovers, busy and timid, flash ahead now
As I follow to scout the edge.

Up to the hermit's view, cool breeze while
Rowans cling constantly to the cliffs, a small flock of pipits rise,
The water below: clear with red gold . . .
The loch wide and dark ahead, like a sea.

The ancient dips of human work are soft laid with grass
Here ash trees bud black off stark rock -
A clump of daffodil shoots reflect gentler times.
The south side shallow, harbour clefts still show.
While the route is inevitably back, breath cool and deep,
Renewed by richness so easily missed.

Bridie Pursey

Contrails

The high white linear contrails score our blue Yorkshire sky bound for sunny beaches, carefree people riding high. And I remember other days when fighter pilots watched their tails and parachutes were blooming, and planes left fiery trails. Summer days when sunny skies were filled with contrails over Kent weaving in the footless wastes many an airy cerement.

Far above the warring land the pike-nosed planes would seem remote from futile earthly strife as figures in a dream. Yet they were flown by mortal men, looking with human eyes into mirrors, probing depths through sun-starred canopies.

They had not long to ride the air this company so gay swooping like monstrous mayflies that live for but one day. They died alone; fell down the sky, trapped amidst searing flame, unknowing of the glory, the gratitude, the fame.

But gratitude and memory alas, have as short a span in the mind of humankind as that of a fighting man. On Battle of Britain Sundays unblooded youngsters laugh at bald, bareheaded veterans who weep at the Cenotaph.

Ronald Womack

The Tup Inn Grand Ball

I don't know if you will believe this,
It almost made me stop and think
As to whether I should go teetotal,
And give up that demon called drink.
This happened to me, late one evening,
As I sat in my big easy chair,
I had been to 'The Tup' for a drink with my pal
And I think I had more than my share;
As I gazed at the mantelpiece before me,
I was feeling more drowsy by far,
For the clock and the ornaments suddenly seemed
Like the gantry behind the pub bar.
In the distance the barman was calling,
Just when the drams felt so fine,
'Come along now folks, drink up please,
It's way past closing time!'
So I lifted my drink and I swallowed it down,
Then shouted a 'cheerio.'
'Goodnight, Margaret, see ya chick.'
Then homewards did I go?
The last of the patrons were leaving the pub,
Margaret stole a wee glance at the clock,
A last look around as she closed the door,
Then turned the key in the lock:
So now the pub was silent,
The minutes slowly pass,
There was not a sound, but wait,
Was that the clink of glass?
And sure enough, up on the bar,
The tumblers started to pair,
And off they went along the top.
As singing filled the air,
The whisky bottles on the shelf,
All shouted one and all,
'Hip hooray! It's time once more,
To hold the Tup Inn Grand Ball!'
And so the band got started,
Behold it was a sight,
While you and I were fast asleep,
They danced away the night.

Onto the floor came the *cognac,*
And the *cointreau*, with her fan,
And kicking their legs high in the air,
They did the French can-can;
The *Bushmills* and the *Guinness*,
Didn't seem to care a fig,
As they turned and twirled around the floor
When they did the Irish jig.
Whyte and *Mackay* and *Johnny Walker Red Label*
Sat back and enjoyed all the scenes,
The *lagers* and the *sweetheart stouts*
Were now the best of freens;
Next came a spot of singing,
The applause brought down the house.
The song they sang was 'Scotland Forever'
The choir, the *Famous Grouse*.

The *Tartan Specials* took to the floor
And started doing their thing,
'Best set in the hall' and 'hoogh' they went,
When they did the highland fling.

Two gatecrashers from *Boddingtons*,
From the land of the Sassenach,
Were ordered to leave by the bouncer,
A bottle - the best - *Glenfiddich!*

Booth's gin and *Bristol cream sherry,*
Crème de menthe and *advocaat,*
Made up a wee circle and did the slosh
And shouted, 'Here's where it's at!'

A six-pack of extra strong *Carlsberg*
Pushed their way onto the floor
And did a stirring display of the polka,
So the crowd all yelled, 'Give us more!'

The glasses and bottles all took to the floor
As the band played 'rock' of a sort
And the spotlight picked out a peculiar sight,
A boogie woogying bottle of *port!*

Then everyone looked at each other
In question, and seemed to be vague,
For nobody knew what the dance was,
'Cept a dimpled bottle of *Haig!*

When the orchestra sounded a hornpipe,
It just made you think of the sea.
Bacardi, black rum and *white rum,*
Did you ever enjoy such a three?

Smirnoff and *Vladivar vodka,*
Were down there among the great throng,
Their acrobatics were a joy to see
And they sang for us the Volga Boat Song.

And so it went on until morning,
The sun was beginning to shine,
So they gathered around in a circle
And they sang 'For Auld Lang Syne'.
The whiskies, the rums and the port wines,
The glasses, the long, short and tall,
Tiredly made their way back to the shelves,
'Twas the end of the Tup Inn Grand Ball.

But maybe they'll meet one more evening,
Just when the drams are feeling fine,
And Margaret is calling, 'Time gentlemen please,
It's a long, long way past closing time!'

Perhaps I had just one too many,
I maybe imagined it all,
Was I really at home in that big easy chair,
Or was I there, at the Tup Inn Grand Ball?

Robert Anderson Kelly

No Wedding Blues

'You've three daughters,' said the insurance man
when they were only tots.
'Believe me, I've got a wedding day plan
That'll help to save you lots.
A few pence a week till they're twenty-one
Will bring you peace of mind.'
We discuss it long, the deed was done.
So useful we were to find.
All three were eager to plight their troth
As soon as they came of age.
Today brides are older and many more loathe
To commit themselves to this stage.

Dressmakers were found, material bought,
The vicar given a call.
A matter of weeks, no time to get fraught.
Friends decorated a hall.

Sausages, sandwiches, jellies and cream,
A home-made wedding cake.
Good-hearted banter, though no special 'theme',
All paid for with no heartbreak.

Mary Jelbart

There Is Beauty Everywhere

Could we perceive this world of ours,
See it in its totality?
What a beauty! What a splendour!
There would be for us to see.
For whether we look here or there,
There is beauty everywhere.

But since our vision is restricted,
We must needs behold in part;
Thus conscious of our limitations
To behold in every art.
But in spite of all we must declare
There is beauty everywhere.

See the artist at his canvas;
See the sculptor at his work;
See each one toiling patiently
In the scenes where beauty lurks.
Perhaps unnoticed, what do they care?
Since there is beauty everywhere.

And though our lives be so dreary,
Any man would be a fool
Who would not admit unto himself
That the world is beautiful:
Or who would not try to share
The beauty that is everywhere?

Bernard McGinty

Mirror

Look at you, standing there!
Your trunk like a silver goddess
Stretching tall and aligned

So small am I by your side
I wish you could see yourself!
For you don't block my view

No! You take me from the task master
Of the mind that whips me
Away from oneness

You are still when you sway
With harsh winds and rain
You live a perfect life

From root to tip, you are whole in joy
When your teardrop leaves fall, you are OK
You wait silently for newness

I wonder, dear tree, if we are one,
Could it be that you *do* see?
That you see yourself through me?

For I see myself through you.

Judith Thomas

And When I Die . . .

When I die,
many people will send cards,
write letters, phone and leave messages,
say how sorry they are.
What for?
That they haven't written since Christmas?
That they forgot my birthday?
That they were too busy?
'You know how it is!'
I wrote to you, all of you,
and each day I waited for the postman
to bring your replies.
They never came.
I got plenty of offers -
for loans,
insurance policies, easy terms for burial services,
but none that asked me,
asked how I was.
I phoned you, and you said,
'Next time, I'll phone you.'
But you never did.

When I die,
people will talk of me.
They will laugh - and cry -
about the old times.
They'll remember the things I said and did.
'She was a character!'
they'll say.
How I would love to talk to you,
now,
about the old times,
the people we knew,
the things we did, the places we went to.

When I die, they'll come in droves to the funeral;
cousins who 'can't travel' because of
arthritis, lumbago,
weak bladders;
friends who are so busy because
*'That is the way life is, these days,
isn't it?'*

How I wish you'd come to see me in my geriatric cell;
brought flowers,
talked and helped me
pass the time;
made me know that these last few years are as precious
to me
as the ones that have gone before.

Gone, but not forgotten?
Forgotten, but not gone.

Eirina Gerrish

Ghost Town

Chewing gum polka dot high street
Shops boarded up and closed
No police to stop the fighting

No theatre, no library, no football pitch
Homeless buskers sing for their supper
Bored children shelter from the rain

Beauty spot blemished with strewn litter
Boy racers and tipsy aunties speed along
The bumpy helter-skelter roads

Brown envelopes pushed under tables
Building plots sold for one pound
Empty houses and overgrown churchyards rot away.

Nia Glyn Williams

That's Life

Times have changed
In oh so many ways
No longer do simple pleasures
Fill our lives.

The stress of modern life
Is affecting us all
Computers have taken over our world
Children don't play anymore
Stuck for hours watching television
And computer games.

Whatever happened to brain power?
The old days
Many of us would like them back
Life was simpler
There was no such word as stress
It was called worry.

Many of us expect too much from life
As long as we have good health
We have everything, so enjoy every day
Life was meant to be lived this way.

Terri Brant

Suffering

There's so much suffering in the world
Sometimes we question why
The little children are starving
And often left to die.

O why do nations fight
And kill and maim and injure?
When all the time they could unite
And help the world to prosper.

Air crashes are on the increase
Tornados and tidal waves
The earthquakes claim so many lives
O who, mankind can save?

The body is often gripped by pain
Its weakness overwhelms us
We wonder why we suffer thus
Then our conscience does condemn us.

But when we look at the centre cross
And the sufferings that Christ bore
How patiently He agonised
All alone in days of yore.

His hands were pierced with nails
A spear plunged in his side
A crown of thorns upon His head
The man of sorrows died.

He died alone to rescue you
And save you from your sin
He only could unlock the gate
Of Heaven to let you in.

Ruth Edgar

Brothers

Adam kicks the ball up high,
I think if he could
He would probably fly.
His energy seems to know no bounds,
From the house I can hear the sounds
Of him and his brother Jamie cry,
'It's a goal!' 'Good save!' Or even 'Good try!'
They make the most of their holiday time,
Going back to school will seem like a crime.
We've had good fun playing and walking,
Soon it will be *keep quiet, no talking*.
Now it won't be long till Hallowe'en's here
With bonfires, toffee apples and ginger beer.
Times to look back on when they are old,
Memories to treasure, to have and to hold.
Forever in their minds and hearts,
Brothers together, never to part.

Anne Moreland

My Daughter

She was a beautiful person, my daughter
Loving, caring, intelligent, hard-working
I enjoyed being her dad.

Pregnant and a tumour in her bowel
She suffered greatly
Not once did she complain.

Therapies were to no avail
Transfusions but a crutch

It was love that was the source of life
Love of her son, her family, her friends.

A light has gone out in my life
Her absence always with me.

Gerry McColl

Birdsong

Hello little blackbird
Perched upon the tree,
Looking as if you -
Have a song for me.
I was feeling lonely
Till I saw you sitting there,
You seemed to know
Just how I felt,
I really do declare!
Now you are singing merrily
And other birds have come
To join in the chorus
In the early morning sun.
Now I feel much better
And I am singing too,
Bye-bye little blackbird,
Many thanks to you!

Hazel D C Powell

Eyes

He came to me in my darkest hours
No more the vista of fields and flowers
My spirits were of deep despair
The wonders of sight no more to share

His gentle touch, his warmth and love
Opened my eyes, I gave thanks above
He led me through the endless night
Turning darkness into light

He's my sight, my sound, my guide through life
Trust and devotion remove all strife
He lifts me up when I am down
My guiding eyes, my friend - and clown!

They tell me his eyes are as brown as mine
His golden hair so silky and fine
But some, with eyes who will not see
Abuse Man's friend - that should not be

Who in this world gives all without needing?
This is a thought we all should be heeding
Time has erased grey mist and fog
My eyes can see through the eyes of my dog.

Jean Cadman

The Cathedral

Through the broken opening
Suddenly the children were seen,
First one, sleeping in the hewn rock,
Then another, and myriads more,
Still, their stunted heads
Horrifying above the meagre grey sheet,
Blurred smudges in the shadows.

The rain fell from the great height
Along the cathedral shafts.
The noise of its splash echoed in the emptiness
For the children filled no space.
They lay small at the base of the columns
Which soared no longer in bright brilliant glory
To a mysterious Presence.
The ribs broke abruptly, harsh and jagged
Against the grey sky whose clouds
Rushed past the space
Where the vault once was.

Ann Hewlett

Spiral Of Existence

Forward and backward, turning in a circle,
To come again to the beginning.
Millennium fever hits the pitch within the rhythm
Of life's sentence returned.

Who, the leader reborn in a different skin?
One of recognition to the voice of the Master,
To the music played again to a different tune?

Seeing backward in time, looking forward,
Seeing again the Holocaust, Hiroshima, Biafra, Afghanistan
But with a different eye.
Seeing this time the glory of Divine ascension
Of the souls who died for us
As the Christ died at the beginning.

Why this generation, why now the guilt?
Lest we should forget, bite now the dust of
Remembrance, and swallow hard.

Now, must be a new beginning.
A love story of gratitude between nations,
An awakening, like unto a dream of a new reality.
Hope, compassion, the desire to help each other
In the passage of time which is the Now.

The greatest love story of all time
All nations united in their love of each other,
And of the Divine Mother of us all;
This exquisite planet we call home,
This Earth, of which we are the guardians.

What greater than the beauty from above
Of our beloved land?
What more caressing than the sun upon our skin,
Or the moon's gentle touch in the silence of
The night?
The soothing waves of the breathless sea, and the souls
Inhabited there; dolphins, whales, and all others
Born into this huge reality of existence.

All these, the most desired in the moment of death.

All this, the backdrop to the most precious moment in life.
The coming together of like minds, like bodies,
In the greatest of Man's gifts:

The creation of new life.

Catherine Hill

The Sun God

The Sun God, possessor of life-giving energy and force,
Riding in the sky on his golden horse,
Bathing the heavens in a radiant glow,
Afraid of no one, friend or foe.

Aware of his power, he struts the skies,
His fierceness and arrogance often belies
The compassion he has for us mortals,
Although he sometimes sulks in his secret portals.

He combats the darkened, thunderous clouds and mist,
Flirts and charms the emerging rainbow and kisses
Her gently, and woos her with sweet song,
Saying, 'together you and I belong'.

With his winsome smiles and emanating rays,
We love him for his promise of happy days.
In his welcome warmth we love to bask,
The sunset beckons as he completes his daily task.

Irene Greenall

Christmas Day 1914

In the midst of war, the time reached 12 at the start of Christmas Day,
A lull in fighting caused a quiet to sweep all noise away,
A truce was called by both sides, to allow the men to rest
And remember a night so long ago, a child was born, so blessed.

A lone voice broke the silence with the carol, 'Silent Night'
And all along the trenches, voices joined in song, not fight.
Both sides raised white flags of truce, in no-man's-land they met,
They shook each other by the hand and enjoyed a cigarette.

Few could speak each other's tongue, but smiles break barriers down,
All of them only lads, but due by circumstances forced to act full grown.
They felt no dislike for each other and puzzled why they had to fight,
They had to endure the cold and wet and fear from morn to night.

Now on this special Christmas night there was a chance to find
That they were, by their age and likes and loves, all of one kind.
A game of football with the foe was enjoyed by both sides now
But all too soon the hours flew by and to war must sadly bow.

Once more the lads shook hands, but this time was to say farewell
Then those in charge made sure their boys were each back safe and well.
The flags of truce were now removed and war resumed again
But for a few hours on that Christmas Day, goodwill and peace had reigned.

Patricia Harris

The Best Things . . .

It's a well known fact of life
Not open to debate
Residing in East Anglia
Comes at a special rate
Folks live well into old age
Finding life worthwhile
Helping one another
With a ready smile
With lots of healthy fresh air
Heaps of things to do
Many places of interest
Some of them free, it's true
Woodland walks, arts and crafts
Busy markets, Fenland drains
Twitching, fishing, cycling
It hardly ever rains
Ducks and deer, birds of prey
Are all here to be found
Mother Nature's made it easy
Just come and look around!

Sue Reilly

Age

'As I understand you are the lady
Who is interested in this job.
Pray, do sit, or you may stand, as you please.
If you do not mind we will write down
A few notes. We need a keen young person,
Able to do the job,
Otherwise we have no objections.
You were a good dancer, were you not?'
'Yes, sir.'
'I do remember that.
Of course, that was years ago.
Where do you live?'
'At number 27, No End Street.'
'Married?'
'Yes, sir, twice.'
'And your age?'
'Twenty-five.'
'Twice as well?'

Victoria E Tejedor

Under Control?

We're trapped in a glass dome - far from home.
Outside the sparrows fly free.

With storms and delays,
Cancellations and queues,
Changing of planes and -
Exchanging of views,
Hours become days -
With still more delays.

Outside in the rain, the sparrows are free.

We've important announcements, security scares.
More thunder and lightning and a shortage of chairs.
Don't go away. Where can we stay?
Everything is under control.

Don't fall asleep, you'll miss change of gate.
Please line up now, it's getting late.
Everything is under control.

Don't move away, there are vouchers for tea,
Please join this queue; the food's all free.
Everything is under control.

It's getting dark, no more flights today,
The sky's quite grey. Where can we stay?
Everything is under control.

Panic and platitudes, chaos and clichés,
Tomorrow is another day.
Where do sparrows sleep?

Dorothy Howard

Hospital August 2009

Footsteps -
Fast, full of purpose
Footsteps -
Slow and sure -
Plastic on plastic

Trolley squeak
Trolley talk
Clattering cups for comfort

Trolley on soft wheels
Stacked panaceas
A pill too far . . .

'How are you?'

'Miserable
Bad tempered
Pain racked'

Oh! One of those days is it?

Trolley time at the open door
'Breakfast'
Mmmmm

'Cornflakes
Bran flakes
Rice Krispies
Weetabix
Allbran
That's it'

'Yes please'
Straight talk
Of 'marmalade toast
Two slices'
'May I really?'
'Tea - sugar?
Orange juice'
'Everything'

I am overwhelmed
Though I crave hospital porridge

The trolley hostess delivers
And marches on with her
Trembling trolley.

Pain shifting
I dream a little
'You've half an hour'
For what?
'Here's a paper flannel
For your wash
They'll come for you'
For what?

I sit ready
Ready for ease of dressing
Which leg goes where? Oh!
A quick arabesque
And all's settled

I am wheeled
Along a quarter of a mile
Of ribbon corridor
Trolleys, footsteps
Hopeful passengers
To eternal life

Destination
Discharge
Outside, a fateful fag area and freedom.

Margaret Adams

Journeying

I sprang from Earth and soared among the planets,
Propelled along by powerful solar winds,
Past Mercury, circling between Earth and Sun,
And Venus, star of morn and eventide -

To Mars, a million, million miles away:
Volcanoes spewing; sandstorms planet-wide,
And then through seas of asteroids to Saturn,
Nestling amid his sheltering moon-filled rings.

Through myriad stars and suns and galaxies,
Each with their satellite moons, I floated on.
I sought an end, a wall, a rock, a limit,
But only found more planets and more suns.

Then through the clouds loomed up the golden gates,
The Gates of Heaven afire with blinding light.
I slid my hands around their golden bars,
Pressing with all my strength against their weight.

I felt them give and pushed with all my might,
Pleading for entry, gathered all my force
For one last try, I shook the golden bars,
Then sank back on my pillow, fast asleep.

Rosemary Harvey